The South African Mosaic II

The South African Mosaic II

A Sociological Analysis of Post-Apartheid Conflict, Two Decades Later

Second Edition

Nomazengele A. Mangaliso

Hamilton Books
Lanham • Boulder • New York • Toronto • Plymouth, UK

Copyright © 2018 by
The Rowman & Littlefield Publishing Group, Inc.
4501 Forbes Boulevard
Suite 200
Lanham, Maryland 20706
Hamilton Books Acquisitions Department (301) 459-3366

Unit A, Whitacre Mews, 26-34 Stannary Street,
London SE11 4AB, United Kingdom

All rights reserved
Printed in the United States of America

British Library Cataloging in Publication Information Available
Library of Congress Control Number: 2017953688
ISBN: 9780761869979 (pbk. alk: paper)—ISBN: 9780761869986 (electronic)

∞™ The paper used in this publication meets the minimum
requirements of American National Standard for Information
Sciences—Permanence of Paper for Printed Library Materials,
ANSI Z39.48-1992

Contents

List of Figures	vii
List of Tables	ix
Preface	xi
Acknowledgements	xv
1 Introduction	1
2 Post-Independence Conflict: Theoretical Perspectives	23
3 Historical Conflict Dynamics	31
4 Research Methodology	45
5 Data Presentation and Analysis: Part I	51
6 Data Analysis And Presentation: Part II	77
7 Summary and Implications of the Findings	89
8 Presentation and Analysis of 2016–2016 Survey Data	95
9 Challenges and Possibilities of Bridging the Historic Socio-Economic Disparities	109
Appendix A: Acronyms of Variables in the Questionnaire	119
Appendix B: List Of Abbreviations: Some Historical Political Parties	121

Appendix C: List of Political Parties Represented In Parliament in a Democratic South Africa 2016	123
Appendix D: Questionnaire	125
Appendix E: 2016–2017 Survey Questionnaire	131
Bibliography	135
Index	145
About the Author	147

List of Figures

Figure 1.1.	South African "Homelands/Bantustans"	3
Figure 1.2.	Provinces of a democratic South Africa	4
Figure 8.1.	Preference for capitalist/free enterprise economic system	97
Figure 8.2.	Preference for part-capitalist/part-socialist economic system	98
Figure 8.3.	Preference for socialist economic system	98
Figure 8.4.	Unskilled foreign nationals discouraged from migrating to South Africa	99
Figure 8.5.	Unless skilled foreign nationals discouraged from migrating to South Africa	100
Figure 8.6.	Scarcity of jobs probable cause of conflict	100
Figure 8.7.	Strong ethnic affiliations probable cause of conflict	100
Figure 8.8.	Support for a President of Mixed Race/Colored descent	101
Figure 8.9.	Support for a President of Indian descent	102
Figure 8.10.	Support for a President who is White	102
Figure 8.11.	If conditions do not improve, whites as a group may be targets of hostility	103
Figure 8.12.	Whites may be targets of hostility because of historical political differences	103

List of Tables

Table 1.1.	Homeland and Ethnic Group	4
Table 1.2.	South African Population Groups: Estimates in Millions Income Distribution Expressed in Percentages	11
Table 4.1.	Participants in the South African Education Program	47
Table 5.1.	Demographic Characteristics of the Respondents Responses: Best Political Ideology	53
Table 5.2.	Responses: Political Ideology That Is Best for South Africa	55
Table 5.3.	Support For Political Organizations By Ethnic Group Expressed in Percentages	57
Table 5.4.	Responses on Economic Systems	59
Table 5.5.	Responses: Hostility Towards Whites	62
Table 5.6.	Responses on Similarity of Values Held by Various Race Groups	65
Table 5.7.	Responses on the support of a President of a different race group	68
Table 5.8.	Crosstabulation of Duration of Stay Abroad support of a President of a different race	70
Table 5.9.	Responses on probable causes of conflict	72

Table 5.10.	Crosstabulation of Duration of Stay Abroad and Ethnic Affiliations	74
Table 6.1.	Responses on Homeland Leadership	78
Table 6.2.	Responses on alignments in conflict times	81
Table 6.3.	Responses on alignments in conflict times	83
Table 8.1.	Demographic Characteristics of the Respondents (%)	96
Table 9.1.	Gini Coefficient	110
Table 9.2.	Inequality in South Africa. Selected Social Indicators	111
Table 9.3.	South African Income Distribution by Race in Quintiles, 1995–2011	112

Preface

Reassessing the Prospects and Challenges of Post-Democratic South Africa

When the death knell began to sound on apartheid in the 1980s, many prognostic analyses about a future South Africa began to be heard. A slew of books hit the bookshelves of many bookstores, and video documentaries hit the airwaves around the world. These books ranged from a graphical depiction of the atrocities perpetrated by the South African system on blacks (Woods & Bostock, 1986), to speculations about the most appropriate socio-political arrangements in post-apartheid South Africa (Adam & Moodley, 1986; Orkin, 1986). Some experts predicted the coming explosion in South Africa and the country's downward spiral on a course of self-destruction, while others hoped for a bright future where men and women enjoyed equal rights and access to all the country's riches. The burning question has always remained: how will the transitional process take place? What burdens will have to be faced? By whom? What do South Africans themselves think about apartheid's legacy in post-apartheid South Africa?

The original edition of the book, *The South African Mosaic: A Sociological Analysis of Post-Apartheid Conflict,* published in 1994, sought to answer some of these questions. The uniqueness about the book is that it is based on research conducted on black South Africans (referred to as historically disadvantaged South Africans) who had been studying overseas, primarily in the United States. As the author indicates, and as pointed out below, being away from South Africa would presumably give the respondents a bird's eye view of their motherland, free from the inhibitions and suspicions they might harbor if they were inside the country when answering sensitive questions that might be otherwise regarded as subversive at home. A range of empirical evidence has demonstrated that the socio-cultural and political encounters individuals experience in foreign lands often bring into sharp relief in their minds issues that are often taken for granted as givens in their own countries. Reflective learning has been noted as one of the key features of studying in different contexts (Dewey 1938, Hopkins 1999). Thus, the alternative lifestyle experienced in the U.S., enabled the respondents to make insightful comparisons with their own motherland. Coming from different regions of South Africa, the respondents brought a fairly representative view of a cross-section of the country's educated blacks. The preferences indicated in this study are imperatives that future policy-makers in South Africa will probably have to contend with if they are to respect the opinions of a majority of blacks.

Although responses on the various topics raised were diverse and widely varied, several interesting findings were uncovered. On the question of a preferred political dispensation, an overwhelming majority of the respondents supported the option of a 'one person - one vote', in a unitary state. Also, a majority of the respondents preferred a mixed economic system for a new South Africa. A majority of the respondents disagreed that blacks would seek to avenge themselves for past unfair practices, however they agreed that if conditions did not improve at a satisfactory pace, whites would be targets of hostility. Another finding of the study was the existence of social and political distance between the various black race groups. Also, whilst there was general agreement on the role of the scarcity of jobs in stimulating conflict, there were significant differences of opinion on the role of ethnic affiliations. This new edition follows up on some of the 1994 respondents. The findings from the survey conducted in 2016-2017, albeit inferred from a smaller sample of the original respondents, are detailed in Chapter 8. To a large extent they corroborate the findings in the 1994 publication. One of the respondents summed up the conditions in post-apartheid South Africa as 'work in progress.' In a way, this is a familiar narrative for most countries still navigating their post-independence years.

Scholars and general readers will welcome this book as a valuable contribution to our knowledge of the more sensitive issues involved in the debate of what constitutes a just society in South Africa. University instructors may find the book a useful resource for graduate courses in African-American Studies as well as in Political Science and Sociology courses. Because of the treatment of the theoretical underpinnings of race, class, and ethnicity at foundational level, particularly in Chapter 2, the book may also be utilized in undergraduate classes as well. Many of the ideas presented in the book were informed over several stages in the course of the author's life.

First, the author had spent several years of her life in the provinces of the Eastern Cape, and KwaZulu-Natal where she was born, lived, was educated, and worked. Like many other black South Africans, she worked her way up through several years of elementary, secondary, and high schooling under the infamous "Bantu Education" system. She later graduated from the University of Fort Hare (South Africa) majoring in Sociology and Social Work, subsequently receiving an honors degree in Social Work. After graduation, she spent time working as a social worker at the KwaMashu Child Welfare Agency near Durban, KwaZulu-Natal. It was there that she realized how limited the services that such agencies could deliver due to the rigid bureaucratic regulations that originated in Pretoria. A few years of working for Unilever in Durban gave her an exposure to the functioning of large corporate conglomerates. The second stage of development that informed the author's ideas presented in this book were the years of her graduate education in the United States, first at Cornell University in Ithaca, NY; and later, at the University of Massachusetts in Amherst, MA. During those years she shared many of the ideas with professors during her course work, colleagues in their classes, and in presentations at various regional and national meetings of the American Sociological Association. Indeed, the origins of the book can be traced back to the dissertation that the author submitted to the faculty of the University of Massachusetts in partial fulfillment of the requirements for her Ph.D. degree, which was granted in 1992. A source of firm guidance in that venture was the supervision from Professor Randall Stokes, himself no stranger to the complexities of South Africa having written on Afrikaner Colonialism (Stokes, 1975).

The last, but not least, stage for the development of the ideas presented in this book were several ongoing conversations the author had with the respondents over the course of six years when she was involved with the South African Education Program's (SAEP's) four-week long Denison University South African Student Orientation Program. Over a period of nine years beginning in 1982, Denison University in Granville, Ohio was the half-way station for approximately one hundred black South Africans of various ethnic backgrounds on their way to studying at various colleges and universities in the United States. When the students requested the inclusion of an orientation program as part of the SAEP, the idea was that it would allow them time to be oriented to the U.S. higher education system as well as enable them to polish up their skills in math, statistics, and writing. A secondary reason was that they could form the kind of camaraderie that was difficult to accomplish in the context of the ethnically divided townships and villages of South Africa. It was through her involvement as co-Coordinator of Residential Life in the orientation program that the author had an opportunity to hold discussions with this cross-sectional group of South Africans and gained many of the insights that informed this book. Many of the conversations she held lasted well into the early hours of the morning, but were characterized by candor and a sense of hope coached in realism.

For a long time, South African blacks had to be content having their opinions voiced for them by "outside" experts or observers who did so from an etic perspective, with no experiential sense of what it was like to live in the townships, to be told what education system is good for them, and to live a life that was essentially dictated by the government from the cradle to the grave. The voices heard in this book articulate their experience from an emic perspective. Most of them, having experienced the hardships of township or homeland village life, spent some years studying and living abroad before returning to the South Africa and witnessed the changes that took place in the years following the historic democratic elections. These men and women are among the best equipped to look back and reflect on challenges that South Africa has had to struggle with in its first two decades of democracy, as well as to project and prognosticate their visions about the country's future. In this book the author shares with us the hopes and aspirations of the respondents. And, in spite of the enormous challenges post-apartheid South Africa has had to face, in the end one senses a ray of hope from a majority of the respondents – a sense that with the right leadership, South Africa can evolve into a country where its prosperity is shared by all its citizenry.

Mzamo P. Mangaliso
University of Massachusetts, Amherst, MA, USA

Acknowledgements

I would like to express my appreciation to a number of individuals and institutions that played key roles in bringing this book to fruition. I thank my dissertation committee while pursuing my graduate studies at the University of Massachussetts/Amherst in the 1990s from which this book evolved, Dr. Randall Stokes, Dr. Lawrence Zacharias, and Dr. Stephen Small. To Professor Stokes, I am thankful for the time he spent editing the earlier drafts of the 1994 manuscript, and patiently reviewing the numerous computer outputs. Professor Zacharias raised pertinent questions and issues on the study, responses to which were potential dissertations by themselves. Professor Small assisted in clarifying some of the terms used rather flippantly in the area of race relations. Singularly as well as a collective, they contributed towards my intellectual development.

Westfield State University provided me with the space I needed to do the necessary research, and begin the writing process during the sabbatical granted to me in the spring of 2016. This institution in which I have served intermittently as Chair of the Department of Sociology, and Professor of Sociology has been my academic home for the past twenty five years. Students and colleagues are a joy to work with.

My gratitude also goes to the Education Opportunities Council (EOC) under Dr. Mokgethi Mothlabi in Johannesburg, the Institute of International Education (IIE) under Dr. David Smock in New York, and the United Nations Education and Training Program For Southern Africans (UNETPSA). The EOC and IIE provided me and several other historically disadvantaged South Africans with an invaluable opportunity to study abroad on scholarship. The UNETPSA later made it possible for me to continue on to study for a doctorate in Sociology with minimum financial burdens.

I am grateful for the rare opportunity given to me by the IIE and Denison University, in particular Dr. Donald Schilling and Dr. Richard Lucier, to serve on the staff of the South African Orientation Program. Through this experience I had an opportunity to engage in ongoing discussions with historically disadvantaged South Africans of various race and ethnic background that left me greatly enriched. I would like to give my special thanks to the Program participants too numerous to name here. Their views are a prominent part of this book. I think as they read the book they will "hear" some of their voices.

I am forever indebted to my South African compatriots studying and living in North America, who allowed me to use their leisure and academic time so I could have discussions with them on the future of South Africa. To those South Africans who later became the sample respondents I can never be thankful enough. Even though some of the questions in the questionnaire were sensitive and uncomfortable, they thought they were worth asking if South Africa was to move on a constructive path to the future. South Africa has a bright future because it has individuals of their caliber. I reiterate my deepest gratitude to the same individuals who still offered their input twenty years later by completing the 2016-2017 survey.

I thank my dearest friend, colleague, and husband, Dr. Mzamo Mangaliso. He has been an ardent supporter of my efforts, social, and academic, including this book endeavor. In his cheerful manner he has always managed to draw the best out of me. I am forever grateful to have him in my life. My daughters Bande and Unati, who have turned out to be amazing adults, have at key moments done a wonderful role-reversal by cheering my efforts. It feels good to have them as fans, unconditionally.

Last, but not of least importance, I thank my beloved and departed parents Ali Francis Godfrey Jordan, and Neziswa Jumartha Jordan. Despite the challenges of raising five children under the apartheid regime, they managed to be good family architects and left behind a good legacy. My father instilled in me values that are central in my life; values that continue to hold me in good stead and which I hold dear. My mother served as my role model and mentor on issues that I will never learn from any book, seminar, or lecture. As parents they continue to inspire me through a different kind of presence, in my heart and mind.

Chapter One

Introduction

In the latter half of the 1980s the transformation of South Africa from an apartheid order to a more equitable system became a crucial area of debate. Academics and activists alike began to engage in creative dialogue to formulate policies and suggest scenarios of how a new South Africa might be structured (Adam and Moodley 1986; Rotberg 1988; Louw and Kendall 1986; Suckling and White 1988). It seemed reasonable to assume that a change in the then apartheid regime would have an impact on society and, therefore, prudent to begin spending some time analyzing the views of South Africans, in particular those who were expected to play an important role in a new and democratic South Africa. This assumption bore fruit in a doctoral dissertation, later published into a 1994 book, entitled, *The South African Mosaic: A Sociological Analysis of Post-Apartheid Conflict.*

The 1994 publication was based on a study conducted on subjects, who were identified as historically disadvantaged, and targets of the apartheid regime. However, despite the ravages of this regime, these individuals had succeeded and gotten an extraordinary opportunity to pursue higher education in colleges and universities in the U.S. A. The current publication entitled, *The South African Mosaic: A Sociological Analysis of Post-Apartheid Conflict, Two Decades Later*, follows up on some of the subjects. In this publication, some of the issues that surfaced in the 1994 study have been retained because of their pertinence, while addressing emerging ones as South Africa journeys into the new democracy.

Before addressing the issue of the new social order it remains essential to highlight three areas in which the legacy of apartheid has manifested itself the most, and to some degree retains this historical formation. *Race* has undoubtedly played a major role in the structuring of the present South African societal hierarchy. The myth of the "chosen race" was a primary preoccupation of the 17th century architects of modem day South Africa, which translated into the ideology that dominated the apartheid regime[1]. Drawing on an extreme fundamentalist Calvinist interpretation of the Bible, the 17th century architects translated the "chosen" race ideology into a rigid master-slave relationship between whites—specifically the Boer-Afrikaners—and blacks (Moodie, 1975; Stokes, 1975; Pomeroy, 1986). Over the years, therefore, race in South Africa became the key determinant of the other areas: <u>status and class.</u>

Whites, as a racial group, formed the high social status group, enjoying honor, prestige and privileges afforded them by virtue of birth: whites have provided all members of the upper-class. Whites, however, are not a homogenous and monolithic group, in that not all of them are wealthy and upper class. There are working class whites, as well as poor whites. However, by virtue of the South African race grouping, whites relative to blacks have been part of an upper-caste group. Next down the hierarchy are the "Colored" people[2] or people of mixed race who, along with the Indian people have enjoyed limited honor and privileges. At the bottom of the hierarchy have been the African people who constitute the majority of the population with little to no honor, and fewer privileges.

Because of their lack of privileges, rights, and status, the "Coloreds," Indians, and Africans have sometimes collectively been referred to as the disadvantaged South Africans (DSAs) or Blacks. Even within this group, however, a middle-class has emerged which, although belonging to the DSA group, has enjoyed some material benefits. The black-middle class itself has reflected the hierarchy mentioned above. The "Colored," Indian and the African middle-classes have been afforded differential privileges, with the African middle-class at the bottom of the hierarchy. In the socio-economic and political sphere, for example, there has been differential treatment of the various black races. "Coloreds" overall have received better education and pay than Indians, the same being the case between Indians and Africans. Also, while historically middle class "Coloreds" and Indians could own property in South Africa, Africans legally were debarred from owning such property. Furthermore, as recently as 1987, all Africans were mandated to carry passes as documentary evidence of their right to be in a particular area. In a society in which the most educated and wealthy of Africans were required under the pass laws to bear such documentary evidence, and also subject to intense discrimination in all major aspects of their lives, the very concept of an African scholar, African intellectual, African lawyer, African doctor, and African business person, placed such individuals in a highly ambiguous and precarious position (Kuper, 1965; Nyquist, 1983). Educationally, and/or materially, the African middle-class could be better off, yet politically still suffer the same oppression and humiliation as the rest of the African group. Politically, therefore, the African middle-class has not been far removed from the rest of the African masses. The legacy of the unequal treatment of the various black groups described above can thus be expected to persist for quite a number of years into the future.

Also within the African group have been *ethnic* distinctions which have been linked to, and accentuated by "homeland" or "Bantustan" policies Briefly, "homelands" are areas to which African ancestry could supposedly be traced, and where all Africans could exercise their rights to self-determination (See Fig. 1.1).

The historical origins of the concept of "homelands" is given a more extensive discussion under ethnicity appearing later in this chapter. Such "homelands" have subsequently been scrapped with the removal of the apartheid regime. The new and democratic South African government has drawn new geopolitical boundaries that are in keeping with a society in transition. Figure 1.2 below shows the nine provinces of the new and democratic South Africa.

This book retains part of the study conducted by the author, and published in 1994. To reiterate, the focus of the study was on a society that was awaiting a critical change with the promise of the removal of apartheid. The central issue explored was how, given the nature and complexity of the South African society, the form of stratification described in the preceding discussion, and codified by apartheid was likely to manifest itself in the future. The book

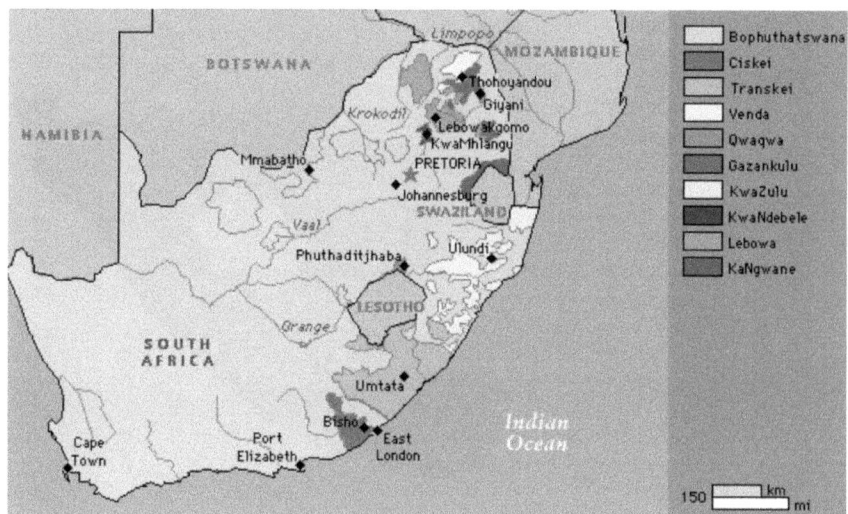

Figure 1.1. South African "Homelands/Bantustans"

Table 1.1. Homeland and Ethnic Group

Homeland	Ethnic Group
Bophuthatswana	Tswana
Ciskei	Xhosa
Gazankulu	Shangaan/Tsonga
KaNgwane/Swazi	Swazi
KwaZulu	Zulu
Lebowa	Pedi/Northern Ndebele
Ndebele	Southern Ndebele
Transkei	Xhosa
Venda	Venda
Qwaqwa	Southern Sotho

begins by pointing out why this issue is of importance. This is followed by an extensive discussion of the latent sources of conflict based on race, status, class, and ethnicity, that were expected to be either intensified or lessened with the removal of apartheid. In chapter two, the sociological literature that identified some of the social, economic, and political conditions that stimulate transitional and post-independence conflict are discussed. Chapter

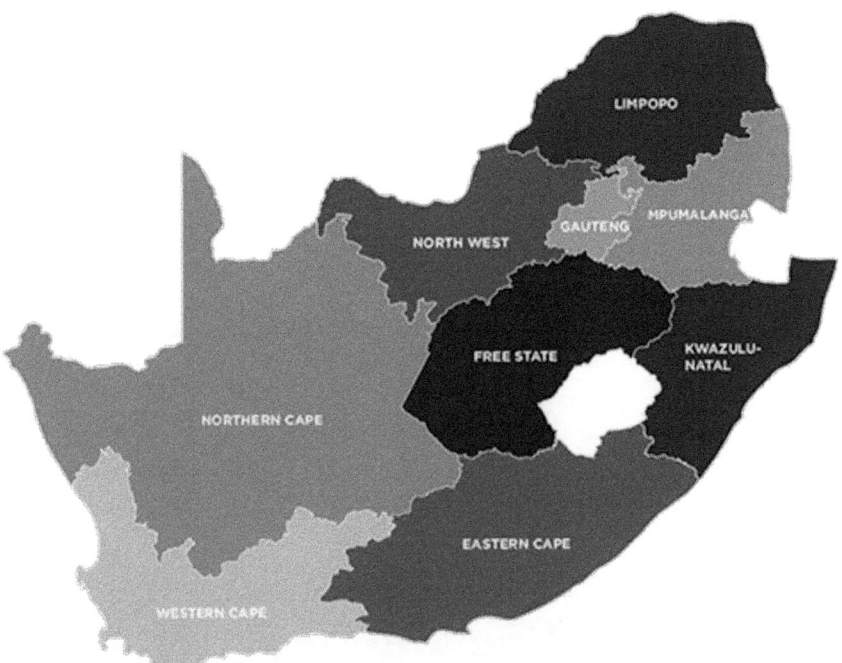

Figure 1.2. Provinces of a democratic South Africa

three identifies conflict dynamics that were in existence in South Africa as the country prepared for transition to a new social order. Included in Chapter three is a discussion of areas of political alignment, and dissention in contemporary South Africa. Chapter four discusses the research methodology, including the sample used to explore the topic of the study in 1994. The responses of the sample respondents were used as a basis for understanding what might happen, or not happen in post-apartheid South Africa. The results of the analysis of these responses are presented in the data analysis and presentation chapters five through seven.

Chapter eight is a discussion, and analysis of the responses from individual subjects recently interviewed and surveyed in 2016–2017 for the new edition of this book. In Chapter nine, the book concludes with a coauthored discussion on the reflections on South Africa as a twenty-two year young democracy as the country continues to strive in the transformation towards a more equitable socioeconomic dispensation.

SIGNIFICANCE OF THE STUDY

Sociological literature indicates that the change period from an old social order to a new one is oftentimes fraught with difficulties and problems. Societies engaged in the process of social, economic, and political restructuring, have often stimulated old and otherwise submerged rivalries and divisions along race, ethnic, class, and religious lines (Furnivall, 1939; Matossian, 1958; Geertz, 1963). In other words, while engaged in the process of building a new nationhood, some societies and governments stimulate or create differences along the already cited lines. Malaysia, Sri Lanka, Haiti, and India serve as useful case studies. The 1994 study focused on potential conflict along race, status, class, and ethnic lines. Data were collected from historically disadvantaged South Africans (DSAs). The primary objective was to determine if the differences within the DSA group would continue into post-apartheid society. In a new social order such differences and distinctions could not be ignored and needed to be addressed. While not intending to elevate differences and divisions, since after forty years of apartheid they could be assumed to exist, the study hoped to indicate areas of potential conflict. If the majority DSA hoped to participate more effectively in a new society, time needed to be spent thinking, debating, and devising means of alleviating destructive conflict, and creating common ground for harmonious social, economic and political participation.

The study was prognostic in the sense that it focused on potential future conflict. Sociological literature in political economy, and social change, seemed replete with studies presenting descriptive analyses of societies (SWAPO, 1981; Stadler, 1987), or studies that gave ex post-facto analyses of societies (Astrow, 1983; Milward, 1984). There was a paucity of studies or literature focusing on potential future conflict. This was understandable since it is much easier to deal with historical facts, or social facts after they unfold. Prognostic studies are difficult since one aspires to make sense of future events that may take a different form from the one anticipated, or future events that may not occur at all. In other words, prognostic studies are susceptible to being highly speculative.

Also, studies focusing on future potential conflict may be unpopular for a number of reasons. Firstly, the struggle against oppression is often conceptualized as essentially that between "they" and "us" (in South Africa being the "black v whites"). Leaders hope that struggles between and among the oppressed will await post-independence. The delay in self-analysis occurs because of two reasons. First, there is the real and justified pre-occupation with removing the oppressor. Second, a critical—albeit objective—self-analysis of the oppressed becomes a hazardous exercise in that the researchers gain opponents who characterize their studies as divisive at a time when there is a call for unity (Sithole, 1980). Be that as it may, it was necessary to engage in discourse about the future of a country undergoing change, in particular one like South Africa where there had been internal strife, economic and political struggling over a protracted period of time. While it remains ambitious to think that any concrete blueprint would come out of this study, it was felt that research on the possible future of South Africa should continue. The future arrived with the removal of the apartheid system, prompting a need to reflect on how far the new South African society has progressed. There is no recipe for a smooth transition to post-liberation, and it is clear that historical conflicts and contradictions appear in the future. It is still hoped that policy-makers, individuals, and scholars interested in the field of political economy, and social change, will find the ideas published in this book cogent and useful.

In the following segment is a discussion of the meaning of the terms that have been used in the South African stratification system.

DELINEATION OF CONCEPTS

Defining any concept that is used to categorize people is never an easy task. Race, status, class, and ethnicity are terms known to have a long history of ambiguity. Applied to the South African situation they have taken a different form. In this book, the author will not dwell too much on formal definitions in case they become too artificial. Instead, race, status, ethnicity, and class will be treated, as they have been known in the South African society.

Race

Definitions of race have included a number of descriptions such as "biological inheritance," "evolution," "blood," "culture," and the "unequal distribution of grace" (Crapanzano, 1986). These definitions are largely arbitrary social constructions that have relied on biology or physical appearance for emphasis. Whatever the definition agreed upon by the apartheid regime, the result has been a romantic-nationalistic philosophy of separate development, which systematically determined a person's rights and privileges on the basis of racial classification.

South Africa's racial classification included four main groups. These comprised the Africans, "Coloreds," or people of mixed descent, Indians, and whites who are of European descent. The political history of South Africa demonstrated clearly that "race," while remaining a categorization based on physical appearance including skin color, hair texture, and facial features, under exploitative conditions became an important element in the formation of the status groups and the socio-economic structure. The structures of racial categorization resulted in the creation of conditions that systematically separated the races—blacks from whites, in order to exclude, exploit, and dominate the former (Magubane, 1979). Consequently, racial oppression and class oppression in South Africa became inextricably bound.

Status

Regarding the concept of status, a Weberian analysis has been found useful. Like "hand me down" clothes, however, it does not quite fit the South African situation. Max Weber (1904) argued that social esteem, prestige, or honor constitute an important part of stratification in society. These factors, according to Weber, constitute status that cannot be reduced to simple economic standing. Weber's use of the term status group includes all instances of cohesive social groups, with their subcultures and their exclusion of outsiders.

On stratification by status Weber argues that:

> . . . status goes hand in hand with a monopolization of ideal and material goods or opportunities. . .Besides the specific status honor, which always rests upon distance and exclusiveness, we find all sorts of material monopolies. Such honorific preferences may consist of wearing special costumes, of eating special dishes taboo to others, of carrying arms . . . (Bendix, 1960; p. 106).

In short the above means leading a specific style of life. Also, status becomes a social-psychological phenomenon in that material conditions determine who enjoys high prestige, deference, and honor. The decisive role of lifestyle means that the dominant status group projects itself, is perceived, and becomes the specific bearer of all "conventions." In other words the dominant status group becomes the standard of all social life against which subordinated groups measure themselves.

The definition of what constitutes high social status in stratified societies, however, is often viewed from the dominant group's point of view while overlooking the view or perspective of the subordinated group (Small, 1989). Frequently, the status systems of the dominant group and the subordinated group are diametrically opposed to each other (Blassingame, 1979). Subordinated groups will sometimes develop their own status systems. These arise from the subordinated groups' position in the social structure, and also gives meaning to their own life. For example, within the African community, which still adheres to some African traditions, older members generally enjoy more honor, are given more deference because of their seniority in the community, regardless of educational qualifications.

One of the contradictions of the South African societal stratification was that by and large, the racial group an individual was born in determined status group membership, thus creating a caste-like situation. Regardless of how educated, and how much wealth and income a member of the disadvantaged group may accumulate, (and there are some wealthy members as mentioned earlier), racial status remains the overwhelmingly important factor. In other words, once race is established status or lack of status, is ascribed.

Class

From a Marxist view, society as a whole is seen as a battleground between the have's and the have-not's, the ruling class/bourgeoisie and the proletariat. Class membership, therefore, depends on whether the individual is an employer, owns and controls the means of production, or whether the individual is a worker. The Marxian class thesis brings forth a number of important aspects. First, it is taken for granted that members of a socio-economic group have an intrinsic tendency to act corporately in support of class interests. Second, the social structure is presumed to be unstable—in due course the lower exploited class is expected to rise up, revolt, and overthrow its oppressors. Third, the class war thesis implies a two-tier model: there is no room for a neutral middle-class and everyone must take sides either with the oppressor or with the oppressed (Leach, 1970). In South Africa a Marxist analysis, while useful, did not quite fit because of the following reasons:

1. While white South Africans enjoyed the largest share of wealth, income, and economic opportunity, they did not all own the means of production. They could, however, control the means of production.
2. "Coloreds" and Indians, who enjoyed some privileges, while not most, did not own or control the means of production.
3. A substantial number of Africans enjoyed virtually no privileges, with a large percentage of them forming the peasantry residing in rural areas under conditions of near poverty. A small middle-class however emerged, and was also encouraged by the government with the primary motive of serving as a buffer between the privileged white population, and the disadvantaged majority in the event of an uprising.

Based on the conditions already described, while a Marxist analysis is useful, these conditions did not very well fit the bourgeoisie/proletariat dichotomy. Also, because race historically has been such a major aspect of people's lives, a class coalition (as conceived by Marx), of the various races was not a given. The point being made about class formation in South Africa, and its contradictions is best discussed by Wolpe (1988). He describes class formation within the white group as more or less comparable to that of other advanced capitalist societies—an economically powerful capitalist class with both monopoly and competitive capitalist portions. Among the black people, specifically within the African group, there being an insignificant capitalist class, a few skilled workers, and a small and relatively underdeveloped petite-bourgeoisie.

Where class structure has emerged within the black population, Wolpe argues, black classes are vastly worse off than corresponding white classes whatever criterion is used to measure them—in terms of capital, wages and income, productive property, and so on. Also, quoting Slovo (1976), he argues that in the case of the black middle strata, class mobility cannot proceed beyond a certain point, and this point is defined in race rather than in economic terms. Objectively speaking, the fate of the black middle class can be linked much more readily with that of black workers and peasants than with their equivalent across the color line (Slovo, 1976).

Another point that needs to be highlighted, and which appears to be a major contradiction, is that although the "Colored" and Indian groups received some concessions from the white government, relative to the African group, they were part of the base upon which white privilege rested. Despite such concessions, at a certain level however they shared a common fate (of being discriminated against) with the African group (Pomeroy, 1986).

Ethnicity

Ethnicity refers to a population that is largely biologically self-perpetuating; shares fundamental cultural values in terms of language and customs that are realized in overt unity; and has a membership that identifies itself, and is identified by others as constituting a category distinguishable from other categories of the same order (Barth, 1969). While race and ethnicity may be mutually reinforcing in the sense that individuals categorized racially may also share a similar culture and language, a distinction between the two concepts may also be discerned. While classifying all peoples by race is empirically questionable in the sense that it can be highly arbitrary, social scientists generally view race as "a category of people who are regarded as socially distinct because they share genetically transmitted physical characteristics" (Robertson, 1987 p. 286). On the other hand, ethnicity generally speaking, refers to the cultural heritage shared by a category of people (Macionis, 1987).

Within the South African context, one may reasonably argue that race, which relied much on physical attributes, intersected with ethnicity or culture. For this reason Glazer and Moynihan's definition of ethnicity was found more descriptive of the South African situation. Glazer and Moynihan (1975 p. 4) defined ethnicity as "all groups of a society characterized by a distinct sense of difference owing to culture and descent." This definition includes difference of culture and descent, real, or putative, of "all groups" in a given society, both minority and majority groups. In the following discussion the various racial/ethnic groups that make up South Africa's current population, both minority and majority will be outlined. Table 1.2 reflects the numbers and percentages of each of these groups.

SOUTH AFRICAN RACIAL/ETHNIC GROUPINGS

Whites

As can be seen from table 1.2, South African whites can be divided into two major groupings, the Afrikaners constituting approximately 60%, and the English, approximately 40%. White South Africans comprise people of diverse origins. However, for the sake of expediency they have been categorized into Afrikaans speakers (specifically the Afrikaners) and English speakers. The origins of the Afrikaner can be traced from the Dutch, the German, and French Huguenots. By virtue of their historical experience, the Afrikaners have been more cohesive than the English group.

The arrival of the settlers in South Africa, ancestors of the present day Afrikaners, began in 1652 when the Dutch East Indian Company established a small refreshment station for its ships at the Cape of Good Hope. These ships were on their way to India, to engage in the spice trade. Although there was no initial intention to establish a colony, the settlement gradually spread. During this period of expansion the settlers encountered the Khoikhoi (Hot-

Table 1.2. South African Population Groups: Estimates in Millions Income Distribution Expressed in Percentages

Racial/Ethnic Group	Number	%	Income
Whites	4.7	8.4%	64.9%
Afrikaners	3.3		
English	1.0		
Other	.4		
Mixed-Race	4.9	8.8%	7.2%
Indians	1.4	2.5%	3.0%
Africans	45.5	80%	24.9%
North & Southern			
Sotho	8.0		
Tswana	7.0		
Xhosa	12.9		
Zulu	13.4		
Other	4.2		
Total	56.5	99.7%	100.0%

Sources: Marger, Martin N. *Race and Ethnic Relations: American and Global Perspectives*, 2015.
Statistics South Africa 2012b. *Income and Expenditure of Households 2010/2011*.

tentots) and the San (Bushmen), collectively known as the Khoisan. It is the Khoisan who engaged in the first wars against this foreign expansion. They resisted the usurpation of their land by means of at least two recorded wars. The first recorded Khoikhoi-Dutch war began in 1659, led by a courageous and determined man by the name of Doman. The Khoisan furiously fought the settlers, destroying food supplies, their farms, and livestock. The second war was waged intermittently between 1673 and 1677, when the Khoisan were finally brought to heel (Mosala and Tlhagale, 1986).

During the early eighteenth century the settlers, now known as Boers—nomadic farmers—began spreading into the interior of the country, until they encountered the Bantu-speaking indigenous people, specifically the Xhosa ethnic group. The earliest recorded skirmishes between the Bantu and Boer was in 1702—exactly one half century after the initial arrival of the settlers in 1652. In various literature, it is argued that it is this long time-span between the arrival of white settlers in 1652, and their first contact with the indigenous Africans (1702) which has provided a basis for the popularization of the thesis that Africans arrived as immigrants on the highveld of the Transvaal at about the same time as the settlers did in the Cape of Good Hope (Davenport, 1977). Recent scholarship has opposed this thesis indicating that there were negroid iron age settlements in the Transvaal as early as the fifth century A.D. thus reflecting an African presence long before white settler arrival (Davenport, 1977). The debate over who arrived first in what is called South Africa now, becomes irrelevant in that it lends no legitimacy to white domination. In other words, the claim by one group to being the first arrivals at a place, does not justify their domination of other groups. At most, it justifies their right to be there.

The contact between the Boers and the Xhosas was, for the most part, hostile, as often typical of frontier periods. The Boers were interested in expansion to new territories, and the Africans were interested in defending their territories. The result of these skirmishes were eight or so wars commonly referred to by the Boers as the "Kaffir Wars," a term that is pejorative to Africans. The Africans referred to the same wars as "The wars of the dispossession of African Land." Needless to say, in the end, because of lack of advanced military technology, the Xhosas were defeated.

As the trekkers moved further northward into the interior, motivated primarily by the desire to control their own affairs, and to move beyond a new British colonial force, they came into contact with two other African groups. The first was the Ndebele group under the leadership of Mzilikazi, who had fled from the Zulu King Shaka's regiments. In a series of skirmishes, the trekkers defeated the Ndebeles and the remaining community fled northward across the Limpopo into what is now modern Zimbabwe. There they carved out a new Matabeleland, where they currently reside alongside the Shona inhabitants (Rasmussen, 1978). The second group was the Zulu group, which had developed a strong military tradition under Shaka's tutelage. Again, after a series of wars against the trekkers, some of which the Zulus won, such as the battle of Isandlwana, the Zulus were finally defeated on the 16th of December 1839, on the banks of the Ncome River. This river was later renamed the Blood River by the Afrikaner government. Ironically, the 16th of December of every year is a declared holiday in South Africa, a day when the current Afrikaners commemorate their defeat of the Zulus. Having defeated the Zulus, the trekkers established a new republic in Natal.

In their trek, the Afrikaners were not only fighting the Khoisan and African forces. The British were also one of their foes. While the trek Boers and the Africans skirmished on the frontiers, the British, recognizing the strategic importance of the Cape for the sea route to the East, occupied that part of South Africa by armed force in 1795. The British annexed Natal in 1843 for similar reasons. The trekkers moved further north, settling beyond the Orange and Vaal Rivers, but in 1848 the British proclaimed sovereignty there also. In the 1850s however, the British lost interest in these territories and granted autonomy to the trekkers (Robertson and Whitten, 1978). The Orange Free

State and the Transvaal were thus established and henceforth referred to as "Boer Republics." To this date, Afrikaners consider the Orange Free State, the Transvaal, and some parts of northern Natal their special territory and heartland.

The new "Boer Republics" were left undisturbed until gold was discovered in the Transvaal in 1886, and in Kimberley which is on the border of the Orange Free State and northern Cape. The discovery of gold attracted both the British and the Africans, and the clash with the British over these territories was renewed. In 1899 a full-scale war exploded. This is the conflict known to the outside world as the Boer War. To the Afrikaners, it is known as "The War for South African Independence" from British imperialism (Hoagland, 1972, p. 26). The Afrikaners, conducting a guerilla warfare against better-equipped, and better trained British troops, however, suffered heavy losses. Later in their history, they would recount how 26,000 of their people, women and children, died in British concentration camps (Hoagland, 1977; Leatt et al., 1986). This twist in Afrikaner lives fueled a dislike of English speakers that continues to this day, and also heightened Afrikaner identity.

In the cities and mining industries the Afrikaners were ridiculed by the British for their poverty, their country ways, and their language. Compared to the English, who were urban and commercially inclined, the Afrikaners were agrarian and poor. The Afrikaners watched as the English gave jobs they also sought to Africans who had been driven from their lands and were willing to accept less pay. According to a South African economist the Afrikaners at the turn of the century "felt themselves pushed around, trampled upon, and humiliated" (Hoagland, 1977 p. 28). By 1930, 300,000 South African whites were defined as poor, and a large number of them were Afrikaners. One of the reasons cited for the apparent Afrikaner backwardness as compared to the English, was their strict adherence and interpretation of Calvinism. In their view, God had taken a direct hand in shaping their social institutions and way of life, thus creating a "sanctified" and chosen society. Thus, living within a sanctified society that God had chosen, and working for the collective Afrikaner group became a powerful force. At the same time, this made for a powerful collective resistance to change (Stokes, 1971). Paradoxically, it is this collective sense that later facilitated Afrikaner ethnic mobilization for seeking political and economic power. Afrikaner nationalism was born as a strategy of ethnic mobilization in order to improve the economic position of the poor and downtrodden Afrikaner. The primary objective of Afrikaner mobilization was to conquer the capitalist system and transform it such that it would fit the Afrikaner ethnic nature. In addition, Afrikaner workers had begun to organize themselves in trade unions to promote their interests against the English capital owners (Leatt et al, 1986). Similar Afrikaner mobilization also occurred on the political front. The 1948 electoral victory of the now defunct Nationalist Party is testimony of the strength and unity of Afrikaner identity against the British. The Afrikaner won exclusive political power and began the systematic exclusion of blacks, while uplifting the previously downtrodden members of their own group.

In the twenty years that followed the 1948 election, the Afrikaners captured 20 percent of the mining industry. In 1968 Afrikaners had 44 percent of all government jobs, a figure that doubled the pre-1947 figure. Also, Afrikaners were securing 44.7 percent of the total national income earned by whites, compared to a 1955 figure (Hoagland, 1977 p. 32–33). By 1980, they shared a 64.9 percent income distribution with other white groups while the entire white group constituted only one-sixth of the South African population (Marger, 2015; Statistics South Africa 2012 b; Wilson and Ramphele, 1989). (See Table 1.2). The Afrikaner achieved economic and political power through a variety of ways. After the 1948 political victory, they gradually purged English-speakers from the top jobs in the police, the military, and the civil service and eventually in major state-owned industries. The establishment of the Afrikaner Broederbond (Afrikaner Brotherhood) was one of the major strategies used to uplift the previously downtrodden Afrikaner. Briefly, the Broederbond was a closed and highly secret Afrikaner association consisting of various power groups that battled for the control of the Afrikaner community, and the direction of the politics of the country. It is an organization that among other activities, strove to preserve not only Afrikaner values of cultural and racial supremacy, but also to exploit the country for the benefit of all sections of its own community, and to improve the economic position of all Afrikaners (Lambley, 1980; Leatt, et al, 1986). The result of the Broederbond's work was a conscious placement of Afrikaners in the nation's major political positions, and the civil service departments. The Broederbond could be characterized as an elite group, within an elite, that engineered South Africa's direction.

Also, the Afrikaners used religious doctrine to buttress their privileged status in South Africa. Again, relying on a rigid Calvinistic interpretation of the Bible, they saw themselves as the "chosen people," culturally and morally superior, and the Africans as intrinsically inferior. Such an interpretation of the Bible thus justified and legitimatized the exclusion of Africans in every sphere of life. Over forty years orthodox Calvinism was preached, and supported by the Afrikaner church, the Dutch Reformed Church. In recent years the same church has denounced this position, citing its earlier position as based on misinterpretations of the Bible. This in itself has been a transformation in Afrikaner thought.

The English-speaking group originating from Britain comprised the English, the Scots, the Welsh, and the Irish. This group also included the English who emigrated from Zimbabwe after it gained its independence in 1980. Historically, the English have occupied and filled the country's major positions in private industries and corporations. In contrast to the Afrikaner, the English put emphasis on differences in class and status rather than ethnic solidarity. In other words, the English have not turned their sense of ethnicity into a political movement in the same manner as the Afrikaners have. While their linguistic and cultural background is important to them, the intensity and salience of their self-identification as English speakers, and their attitudes towards other groups varied by such factors as socio-economic status, education, and age (Nelson, 1980).

Studies on English-Afrikaner relationship have produced divergent results. Some analysts suggest that more Afrikaners than English speakers are prepared to accept in their social circles persons of a similar stratum from the other ethnic category. Other research indicates that middle and upper income English speakers are more status conscious than Afrikaners and consider themselves closer to well off Afrikaners than to English speakers of lower income status. Whatever the results of the various studies indicate, some observers have reported that ethnic distinctions between the Afrikaner and English speaker, long emotionally and politically charged, some dating back to the historical Anglo-Boer war (Leatt, et al, 1986), have not been wholly overridden by similarities in income, occupation, and lifestyle (Nelson, 1980). In other words, the Afrikaner and the English groups do not form a monolithic class in which ethnic differences are irrelevant. However, for purposes of economic and political survival against a black majority, the Afrikaner and the English have formed an alliance. While it is difficult to gauge with accuracy political party affiliation of the English, a general sentiment shared by most blacks is that the then Nationalist party drew some of its support from this group as well as from other small white groups, which is why party managed to stay in power for over forty years. While Afrikaners have been blamed for implementing discriminatory policies, the English quietly supported and enjoyed both the Nationalist Party and the fruits of its policies (Sookdeo, 1991). As R. 1. Neuhaus observed, Afrikaner members of the Nationalist party "resented the fact that the English derived benefits of apartheid, without bearing the political and moral odium of it" (Neushaus, 1986, p. 68).

Other parties that have been linked to the English group are the United Party (UP), which was the principal opposition in the 1950s, the New Republic Party (NRP), the Progressive Federal Party (PFP), and the Democratic Party (Gutteridge, 1990). (See the list in Appendices B and C of some of the major political parties). In general, the racial policy of the English political parties advocated for an extension of the francize to all "civilized" people regardless of race. However, these parties were also quick in emphasizing their loyalty to white interests (van Vuuren, et al, 1987). Overall, the white electoral process excluded blacks, and was thus perceived by blacks as a non-event, totally irrelevant in their lives, and without any positive outcome.

A minority of the white population is made up of the Germans, French Italians, Greeks, and Portuguese who left Mozambique after the 1974 independence. Also included in this group are South Africans of Jewish descent. The first Jewish arrivals came from England and northwestern Europe. Some migrated from Germany in the 1930s and 1940s. However, the greater bulk are of East European descent (Nelson, 1980). One of the strategies adopted by the apartheid government was also to search for new recruits from Hungary (South Africa Now, 1990). The role of these minority groups in the political arena was less clear. However it was reasonable to assume that they were in a highly circumscribed position, in that despite their lack of political clout against the Afrikaner, they had to preserve their self-interests as whites.

DISADVANTAGED SOUTH AFRICANS (DSAS) OR BLACKS

"Coloreds" or People of Mixed-Race

Persons defined as "Coloreds" can be traced from mixed origins. Their ancestors include enslaved people imported from Malagasy, tropical Africa, Southeast Asia, local Khoikhoi (Hottentots) and San (Bushmen) (Crapanzano, 1986; Nelson, 1980). For simplification, "Coloreds" have been defined as individuals who have black and white ancestry. As a result of their heritage "Coloreds" are a diverse group comprising those who appear to be almost white, and those whose physical appearance resembles the Africans. While the "Colored" way of life, and culture is similar to that of whites—most speaking a European language, usually Afrikaans, followed by English—they have, nonetheless, been denied most of the privileges that whites enjoy. Conceding the diversity of the "Colored" group, the South African government set up a number of subcategories defining them in a variety of ways. These included Malays, Cape Coloreds, Griquas, and so on, as well as a convenient "Other Colored" subcategory (Hoagland, 1972).

The majority of the "Coloreds" reside in the Western Cape and maintain an exclusiveness of their own. It needs to be emphasized that cultural exclusiveness in the South African society is not unique to any particular group, but is a unshakable phenomenon resulting from legalized and forced geographic separation of the various population groups.

As can be expected, how governments define people is sometimes at odds with how they define themselves. A prominent "Colored" leader for instance defined a "Colored" person as "one who is discriminated against in a particular sort of way" (Hoagland, 1972, p. 104). Also, over the years, the number of "Coloreds" who rejected the use of such a term increased, the use of the term black being the most preferred, particularly by the most progressive and political members of this group. The use of the term black was strongly advocated by the Black Consciousness Movement (BCM). One of the achievements of BCM was to enable "Coloreds," Indians, and Africans to see themselves as a single black group on the receiving end of apartheid.

However "Coloreds" have been defined, or define themselves, as mentioned earlier in this chapter, they have been part of the intermediate community, receiving preferential treatment from the dominant white group relative to the Indians and Africans, yet at the same time, suffering various forms of discrimination. One can realize that apartheid put "Coloreds" in an ambiguous position. Various studies in the literature indicated some degree of apprehension among "Coloreds" about their fate should the African majority come to power (Hoagland, 1972; Lambley, 1980; Nelson, 1980). While they secured some privileges during the apartheid years, these privileges could not be guaranteed after the removal of apartheid with a government under African rule.

Indians

In the literature, the Indian population has been characterized as a middleman minority (Turner and Bonacich, 1980; Arkin, 1981; Klein, 1990). Turner and Bonacich (1980) defined middleman minorities as migrants in a recipient society, who maintain distinct cultural traits, live in separate sub communities, cultivate high degrees of internal solidarity through kinship ties, endogamous marriages, and as a rule avoid politics unless their interests are affected. Pachai (1971) argued that by and large most Indians would care more for economic improvements than for political power. Also, according to Zenner (1982) the most distinguishing trait of middleman minorities is that a substantial and disproportionate number of its members are engage in small commercial enterprises. Another important telling factor of middleman minorities is that oftentimes they find themselves in between a superordinate minority group, and a subordinated majority group in the stratification system. This position then manifests itself in strained relations with both the superordinate minority, and the subordinated majority group. These descriptions, it can be argued, generally fit the South African Indian case.

Indians originally migrated to South Africa in 1860, either as indentured laborers to work in the Natal sugarcane fields, or as passengers who migrated of their own free will in 1872. Most of the indentured laborers chose to migrate to South Africa because of problems they had in India, such as low caste, breaking of caste prescriptions, family squabbles, and for the most part promises of economic prosperity by recruiting agents (Kuper, 1960; Meer et al., 1981). The immigration of both the indentured and passenger Indians was halted by law in 1913 and indentured laborers in particular were granted their freedom from their contracts (Meer, 1969; Bradlow, 1978; Nelson 1980). Henceforth many individuals from these two groups decided to make South Africa their home.

Initially, a distinction could be discerned between the two Indian groups as depicted in the following statement:

> Generally, passenger Indians came from a higher standard of living in India than did the indentured; they wore better apparel, enjoyed a higher degree of education, and ate better food. The passenger Indians kept up their links with their ancestral home by constant communication in writing and in person and preserved their exclusiveness by the importation of wives from their own villages and castes (Kuper, 1956, p. 129).

Indentured laborers, on the other hand were relatively less educated, and for the most part unable to keep communication channels open with relatives in India. Whereas an ethnic bond could have been established among indentured laborers because of the experience of travelling and working as indentured laborers, an ethnic bond was vital to the passengers for economic reasons (Klein, 1987).

Currently, of the Indian South African population, about 10-15 percent is of passenger origin, the remainder being of indentured origin. Of the passenger migrants, 60 percent are Muslim and 35 percent are Hindu. Of the indentured origin, approximately 80 percent are Hindu, and most of the remainder being Christian and Muslim (Klein, 1987). Whatever their origins, or their earlier activities, in contemporary South Africa, approximately 90 percent of the Indians are urban, have formed an educated middle-class, many have started businesses and proved to be skilled entrepreneurs despite racial discrimination (Moodley, 1976).

Although some Indians have played a prominent role in South African politics as depicted by Mahatma Ghandhi[3], relations with the African majority, particularly in Natal, where the majority of the Indians have found home, have been problematic. For the most part, Africans have been unevenly distributed in the ranks of the marginalized and menial occupations. In contrast, Indians not only dominate a considerable portion of the retail industries, they also fill most of the supervisory positions in the province's economy. This situation resulted in Indian-African conflicts, which in some years culminated in physical violence. The historical, and the worst, is the 1949 conflict when disgruntled Africans indiscriminately attacked Indians. Similar conflict also occurred in the mid-1980s particularly around the Inanda Durban area where Indians and Africans lived in close proximity.

Africans

Africans who are the indigenous people of Africa, constitute the majority of the South African population. South Africa's African population belongs to a number of ethnic groups. On the basis of cultural and linguistic affinities they can be divided into six major groups, which are: Shangaan, Sotho, Ndebele, Venda, Xhosa, Zulu. However, within these major groups are subgroups. For example, the Sotho group comprises the Northern Sotho (Pedi), Southern Sotho (Shoeshoe), and Western Sotho (Tswana). The Shangaan include the Tsonga. The Zulu group includes the Swazi and the Ndebele. The latter, unlike the Zimbabwe Ndebele who are a Nguni or Zulu offshoot, have been variably influenced by the Sotho language and culture. The Xhosa group includes the Thembu, the Bhaca, the Mfengu, the Mpondo, and other smaller ethnic groups.

Historical literature indicates that the various African groups engaged in combat among themselves before the advent of the white settler (Mutwa, 1969; Thompson, 1972; Peires, 1982). Combat, however among the African groups was of a different nature than the one engaged in against the white settlers. The purpose of war was not the destruction of productive resources, but their acquisition and absorption, including both property and human individuals. In other words, the objective of war was one of conquest and the assimilation of the defeated group by the victorious group. Frontier wars with the white settlers were of a different nature. While the settlers were concerned with the acquisition of land, the indigenous people were concerned with preventing the appropriation of their land. This conflict obviously was originally over a clash of economic interests and not over skin-colors. To describe this initial conflict primarily in racial terms would be to imply that the indigenous people would have easily acquiesced in the appropriation of their land if only the expropriators were of similar racial origin to themselves (Mosala, Tlhagale, 1986). However, the fact that the out-group members with whom the settlers were competing, were of a different race and culture ultimately turned the struggle into an economic and racial conflict. Not only were the defeated groups legally subjected to the victors, psychologically they were rejected, and expelled from the desired or conquered territories. Said differently, the defeated groups were not incorporated into the "victors" society. Also, to prevent a possible alliance between the various African groups, any blurring divisions between these groups were revived and their differences, reconcilable or irreconcilable, were re-emphasized (Pereis, 1982). The sole aim of highlighting these divisions was to discourage any form of alliance among African groups that could pose a threat for white settlers. Conversely, among the white ethnic groups cultural differences were whitewashed and de-emphasized as evidenced in Afrikaner-English differences, with the sole purpose of political survival against an African majority.

Promoting cultural differences among the African groups is a strategy that worked well for the ruling Afrikaner government. Whilst there are cultural variations amongst the African groups, the Afrikaner government used this strategy to legitimize the concept of separate development and affording a privileged position to most white South Africans. South Africa's policy of separate development, of which homelands were a major component, culminated in designation of ten land areas as homelands for the various African ethnic groups. (footnote homelands and resource). Most homelands, while containing places of traditional significance to respective ethnic groups, reflected historically distorted boundaries. Most citizens, and African leaders, both traditional and modem, regarded homelands as illegitimate in that they were drawn arbitrarily by the Afrikaner government, without consultation with legitimate African leaders, solely for political ends and expediency.

SUMMARY

All in all, Afrikaner ascendancy to political and economic power produced a society distinctly separated along race lines with each racial group receiving differential treatment. Also, there was purposeful encouragement of African ethnic groupings put into practice through the establishment of "homelands." The homeland scheme produced a society where South African nationals were considered to be whites, "Coloreds" Indians, and those Africans who were born in urban areas. Curiously, these South African nationals enjoyed differential rights and privileges as citizens. In the next chapter, sociological and other related theories that focus on the conditions that stimulate transitional and post-independence conflict are reviewed.

NOTES

1. Literally translated from Afrikaans, apartheid means separateness. It is a government system based on the separation of various races and resulting in the differential treatment of such races. While apartheid is conventionally regarded as having been introduced following the electoral victory of the Nationalist Party in 1947, it has a precursor in segregation that dates back to the era when the English were in power. History indicates that segregation was the outcome of British imperialist thought. The Afrikaner Nationalist Party government codified segregation by taking it to its

logical conclusion. For details on this conjecture see John W. Cell (1982), and that Saul Dubow (1989).

2. In this study the terms "Colored" and Mixed-race will be used inter changeably. The writer realizes that the term "Colored" is becoming widely less acceptable. For this reason, throughout the study it will be put in quotes. The writer could not get rid of the South African race terminology. The use of the term "Colored" should therefore not be construed as reflecting the writer's acceptance of it.

3. Mahatma Gandhi arrived in Durban South Africa, in May of 1893 from India. A barrister by profession, Gandhi had come to conduct a lawsuit in the then Transvaal. Mahatma Gandhi experienced the humiliation of racial discrimination first hand when he was thrown out of a first-class train couch while travelling to the Transvaal. From then, he was made aware of the plight of the South African Indian, and started mobilizing Indians citizens to fight for their rights. Although Gandhi's movement initially was concerned with only the plight of the Indians in South Africa, in subsequent years Indian political organizations formed alliances with the Africans as depicted in the Xuma-Naicker-Dadoo pact of 1947. This pact emanated from a 1943 South African Indian conference, where one of the resolutions arrived at was exploring ways of achieving closer co-operation with the Africans. The pact, finally achieved in 1947, included Dr. Xuma, of the African National Congress, Dr Naicker, of the Natal Indian Congress, and Dr Y.M. Dadoo of the Transvaal Indian Congress (Bhana and Pachai, 1984).

Chapter Two

Post-Independence Conflict
Theoretical Perspective

History abounds with cases indicating the difficult period societies have gone through after gaining independence from external, and/or internal group domination. During the transition to independence, and after independence the future for most countries remains unstable and uncertain. Some countries eventually attain stability, then move into gradual economic growth, and finally shift towards the desired democracies. However, this stage is reached after a protracted period of political and economic strife, and also after many set backs which may culminate in military dictatorships, violent revolutions, counter-revolutions, and civil wars. While there have been "success" cases such as, Botswana, Malaysia, and others, the period after independence for some countries, has been one of indefinite trial and error. Haiti, Nigeria, Philippines, Uganda, and Sri Lanka are cases in point. In this chapter the literature addressing conditions that create perpetuate conflict well after independence is discussed. Where applicable, such conditions are directly linked to the South African situation. As South Africa goes through the transition period from apartheid rule to a new democracy, it can be expected to go through its own difficult and challenging period. The challenges that South Africa may have to deal with may center around some of the following issues: the role of the state and its use of national symbols, finding common ground and encouraging pluralism, discouraging primordial sentiments, dealing with fast rising expectations, and the problem of race/ethnic relations. The issues are analyzed in the following discussion, beginning with the role of the state.

THE ROLE OF THE STATE

In South Africa, since the state has played a highly visible and instrumental role in the creation of a societal hierarchy, it makes sense that a discussion on possible future conflict should begin with an analysis of the state. Lenin (1917) in his historical analysis of the state, asserted that:

> the state is the product of society at a certain stage of development; the admission that the society has become entangled in an insoluble contradiction with itself, and that it is cleft in irreconcilable antagonism which it is powerless to dispel. But in order that these antagonisms classes with conflicting economic interests may not consume themselves and society in sterile struggle, a power apparently standing above society, but placing itself above it, and increasingly separating itself from it, is the state (Lenin, 1917; p. 8).

In South Africa, in particular, the state has functioned as an instrument of social control. To carry out this function the state has relied heavily on the use of the army and the police in controlling and governing the oppressed classes. Not too long ago the South African government referred to anti-apartheid political movements, specifically the ANC and the Pan Africanist Congress (PAC) as "terrorists" who were communist inspired. The army and the police thus viewed such political groups as the "enemy" to be fought and destroyed. However, with the reforms instituted by the then President De Klerk, the same political groups got invited to participate in the discussions about the future of the South African polity. The greatest challenge was reeducating both the army and the police to support reforms that included former "enemies."

The stability real or illusory of any society depends to a large degree upon the effectiveness and the legitimacy of the state and the political system. While effectiveness is instrumental, indicating the actual performance of the state, and ability to achieve desired goals, legitimacy is evaluative and highly subjective. Groups regard the state as legitimate or illegitimate in so far as its values fit, or not fit with theirs. Societies may, therefore reject a state and its political institutions not because it is ineffective, but because its symbolism and basic values negates their own (Lipset, 1960). Lack of legitimacy, therefore, increases the cost of domination (Adam, 1985) as states attempt to impose and coerce people into accepting dominant values and symbols.

The situation described above existed in South Africa. The apartheid government was effective in achieving its desired goals, no matter harmful those were to certain segments of society. However, its legitimacy as a government had long been a matter of contention, because it did not represent the values and symbolism of the majority of the people, and because it was not based on shared beliefs. It was thus reasonable to argue that a new government that would be in place after apartheid, would find itself faced with a similar problem—that certain groups (racial, political, cultural, etc.) might perceive its values and symbolism as negating their own.

The use of symbols plays an important and dual role in the configuration of new societies and political systems. Symbols help to legitimate those in power and also to mobilize previously uninvolved civil society into participation in political life. In addition, symbols can assist in changing some perception on critical issues. In other words they can be used to neutralize past experiences and build bridges between the past and the future (Valera-Guinot, 1990). At the same time the use of symbols may be a source of alienation for some societal groups in particular those groups who perceive a negation of their own values.

Since modern societies cannot exist without some form of state government,[1] class antagonism can be expected to be present in most societies, including newly independent societies with South Africa as a case in point. Members of any newly elected government by definition become the ruling class. Also, the state holds the key to a wide range of economic and political benefits that it distributes by some internally determined process. Because of this function the state is therefore in a powerful position to affect the livelihood of a number of groups and communities. However, in carrying out the distribution and policymaking functions, the state is not necessarily a neutral or passive actor. As already indicated, political power inevitably creates a privileged position for those who exercise it. Such privilege may be reflected in the manner in which the state becomes an autonomous body that possesses its own interests and objectives, independent from the rest of the populace. Such interests may range from preserving power, especially that of its bureaucrats, to serving favored, and powerful groups. The continuance of the state thus relies heavily on how legitimate, and fair it is perceived to be in the eyes of the citizenry. If not, attempts to overthrow and replace it may begin to surface.

FINDING COMMON GROUND

Plural societies present a special challenge. A notion introduced by Furnivall (1939), he defined a plural society as "comprising of two or elements or social orders which live side by side, yet without mingling in one political unit" (Furnivall; 1939; p. 446).

Furnivall's definition of plural societies fits the South African case. Some of the bases of plural societies include different racial groups, difference in language, religion, and custom. In his studies of plural societies Furnivall observed that the rulers and the ruled were of different races, and lived apart from one another in separate communities. Observing that each community possessed a distinct set of values, sometimes incompatible with those of other cultural groups, he characterized a plural society as one lacking consensus, or, in his terms, one without "common social demand" (Rabushka and Shepsle, 1972 p.). To offer some concrete examples, in a plural society the installation of a historical monument may provide benefits for one racial group and none to the other groups. In point of fact, some groups may find an installation of a monument alienating or an expression of hostility against their own existence. The existence of some of the historical holidays recognized in South Africa are another example in that they continue being a constant reminder of historical battles and conflict. Whether such holidays will remain part of the official calendar in a new social order remains a challenge.

DISCOURAGING PRIMORDIAL SENTIMENTS

In order to establish common ground, and group consensus, newly independent governments may have to discourage, and subordinate what Shils (1957), and Geertz (1963) referred to as "primordial sentiments."[2] This task involves discouraging loyalties to subnational cultural groups since such loyalties have the potential of undermining political stability. It means that the state must attempt to develop a single polity out of disparate ethnic groups brought together by the vagaries of history. Making the process work tests not only the state's abilities at consensus building, it also involves a kind of social learning in which the whole society must participate (Smolicz, 1988). Herein lies the problem in that some groups within the plural society may perceive consensus building as their own destruction, particularly if it entails negotiating away some of their demands. Negotiable, and non-negotiable demands are evident in most stratified societies. Negotiable demands are those that normally cluster around power sharing, recruitment, and distributional issues. Non-negotiable demands cluster around subjective issues, the more emotionally laden ones of identity, survival, self determination, and status. In other words, if in the process of consensus building, a specific group perceives a reversal of what it values in terms self definition, and a perceived reversal of group prestige, status, and honor, demands are likely to be non-negotiable (Rothchild, 1986). A defeat in claiming non-negotiables, consequently, leaves many losers stewing in humiliation, craving for vengeance, and waiting for a new round of confrontation. This sentiment is expected to persist in a new and democratic South Africa.

On the other hand it may be possible to create new societies that emphasize national unity, and at the same time recognize diversity. In other words, societies can be created which allow a unity in which the principle of diversity also finds full fruition, thus enabling different societal segments and communities to follow their own customs and usages (Sharma, 1988). This is the road that political activists and government officials (The New York Times International, 1990; Economist, 1990) explored for a new South Africa.

THE ROLE OF OTHER INTEREST GROUPS

In plural societies, while the state serves as a force influencing the social processes that encompass different groups, the state also becomes a resource that the different groups compete for (Skinner, 1975; Brass, 1985). In South Africa, for example, several political parties can be expected to continue contending for power sharing. Also, the trade union movement that has always had a strong voice in representing the interests of the black workers and their political ideologies will be agitating for power sharing.

DEALING WITH RISING EXPECTATIONS

Independence is often followed by expectations for change in social, political, and economic relationships that characterized the old social order. However, such change may not come soon enough for some segments of society. The expectations of groups that have been historically disadvantaged may rise at a faster rate than the existing political, economic, and social institutions can absorb them. Unmet expectations, in turn, may result in political violence caused by the frustration of those groups who suffer from relative deprivation, in other words, those groups who perceive their conditions not to have improved relative to other groups. Writers as disparate as Karl Marx (1848), Paul B (1957), and Harry Magdoff (1978), have argued that political power will always gravitate into the hands of those who possess economic and social power regardless of political institutions and ideologies. The challenge for governments is to make certain that social, economic, and political power eventually gets widely distributed among the people in a multitude of institutions and at all social levels (Douglas, 1972).

So far the above challenge remains unmet in most countries, including the newly independent, and developing countries. Disparities that existed before independence linger on long after independence, resulting in the alienation of certain segments of society. A future South African government will be faced with a similar problem. The ANC, in particular, represents diverse groups of people. These groups range from the uneducated and probably impatient township youth on one end of the spectrum, to the educated liberal white South Africans on the other end. Whether the needs and interests of these diverse groups can be met in a manner that appears fair and equitable remains a challenge. To begin with, most white South Africans favor the continuation of capitalism, whilst many black South Africans including most of the township youth have equated capitalism with apartheid or white domination, and thus favor some form of socialism, or mixed economy. Black South Africans generally do not believe that racial inequality can be adjusted without state intervention, in other words, they do not believe that existing economic imbalances will be corrected if left to free market competition (Third World Quarterly, 1987). The sentiment expressed by black South Africans about capitalism is logical if one looks at its historical significance. Capitalism is an economic system that exploited blacks and gave them very little. In a future South Africa, most blacks would like to see this condition avoided, if not reversed. In other words, an economic system that promises to improve the well being of all South Africans is preferred, at least by most blacks. In a new South Africa this is a contested terrain. Former President Nelson Mandela for instance, on his release from jail strongly advocated for the nationalization of the country's major industries. Ironically many of these had been nationalized under the ruling apartheid Nationalist government. These included air transportation (SAA), railroad and shipping industry (SAR&H) the postal services (GPO), the electrical supply industry (ESCOM), the military manufacture (ARMSCOR). The mining industry was highly concentrated in the hands of a few corporations, such as Anglo-American Corporation.

However, facing strong opposition both nationally and internationally, Mandela was forced to modify his stand, and instead, emphasized the nationalization of a few select industries like the mines.

THE PROBLEM OF RACE/ETHNIC RELATIONS

In South Africa, the black vs. white fracture has always been a given and taken for granted as part of the formation of that society. The African vs. "Colored" vs. Indian divide has not overtly manifested itself because these groups have over the years come to view themselves as part of the DSAs. Their unity has been based primarily upon the existence of a common foe in the form of apartheid. However, because of the separation of the various race groups, lack of knowledge about each other resulted in subtle discomfort and lack of real trust between these groups. In other words, once the common enemy was removed some fracture was expected between the African, "Colored" and Indian group. Also, since ethnicity has been kept alive, and encouraged through the allocation of homelands for Africans, ethnic divisions were expected to surface, the Zulu-Xhosa divide being the most dominant. Any new government coming to power in a new South Africa had the challenge of either dissolving the existing compartmentalization of society, or encouraging the establishment of linkages that cut across such compartments.

SUMMARY

In summary, most newly independent societies face the task of resolving differences and problems emanating from the old social order, while confronting newly arising problems. Since such governments are in the process of creating a new society, problems are bound to come up that are characteristic of experimental periods. The prime objective of such societies, and their governments, including the new government formed in South Africa, was to learn through trial and error, to learn from other societies that had gone through a similar history, while striving at maintaining political and economic viability. In the next chapter a more extensive discussion is given of the dynamics that were already in existence as South Africa transitioned to a new democracy.

NOTES

1. Marx and Engels' advocacy of creating societies in which the state government would no longer be a necessity, and thus "wither away" has proved to be illusory. Socialist governments which were formed with the purpose of turning the means of production into public property, and in the process make the existence of the state government unnecessary; have themselves turned into a ruling class that enjoyed more power and privileges than the rest of the populace.

2. Geertz (p. 109) developing a concept introduced by Shils described "primordial sentiments" as sentiments that stem from the "givens" of a culture or social existence. These "givens" arise from being born into a particular social group speaking a particular language, or sharing common beliefs, and following particular social practices. These congruities of blood, speech and custom are seen to have an ineffable and at times an overpowering coerciveness in and of themselves. One gets bound to one's kinsman, one's neighbor, one's fellow believer not out of personal attraction, absolute necessity, common interest, or incurred moral obligation, but in great part because of some unaccountable absolute importance attributed to the very tie itself.

Chapter Three

Historical Conflict Dynamics

In this chapter, conflict dynamics that were in existence in South during the apartheid years are highlighted and discussed more extensively. These are problems that were expected to take center stage because they were created and accentuated by many years of apartheid rule. To the author's mind, their shift to the center stage would be a natural progression from having removed a common or old enemy in the form of the apartheid regime. In this chapter, also views shared with the author by South Africans through informal interviews on areas of concern are presented. These views were later used as a base from which the questionnaire in the 1994 study and publication was drawn. The chapter ends with the research questions that helped in guiding the 1994 study.

WHITE SOUTH AFRICANS

The Afrikaners

It is often argued that white South Africans, specifically the Afrikaans speaking whites, have over the three hundred years of their residence in South Africa cut off links with their Western European countries of origin. As a result, Afrikaners perceive themselves as legitimate inhabitants of Africa, and lately refer to themselves as the "white tribe" of Africa (Cronkite, 1987; Malan, 1990). Any challenge by any race internal or external to the Afrikaner ideology of white supremacy would be met with resistance and a retreat to the "laager" or war mentality, characteristic of the frontier period when they fought English and African forces.

No doubt the Afrikaners will not be leaving South Africa, at least not in large numbers. They have no "motherland" to go to, and perceive themselves as the white tribe of Africa, "a people tough enough to stake everything on the Dark Continent and survive" (The Economist, 1990; p. 13). In South Africa the white urban working class—the Afrikaners specifically—are in a vulnerable position. While better educated relative to blacks, and protected from competition by discriminatory racial laws, this is a privilege they were not expected to have in a future South Africa. As already mentioned in the preceding chapters, one of the major goals of apartheid was to protect the large number of whites (mainly Afrikaners), who would be at risk from competition with blacks. A large number of them were thus expected to vociferously resist any possible black competition. Since the majority of Afrikaners had limited options to go anywhere in the world, they were expected to stay in South Africa, resentful and potentially dangerous towards a black majority.

Currently, a minority of Afrikaners has made strong overtures towards establishing a homeland for whites, specifically Afrikaners. At a meeting in August 1988, held at the Institute of South African Race Relations, Professor Carel Boshoff, leader of the Afrikaner Volkswag, outlined the argument behind the call for an Afrikaner homeland. He argued that political-power sharing with blacks would have far reaching implications for the Afrikaners, as the protection which they enjoyed as a minority group with absolute power would be eroded. He argued then that Afrikaners should have the right to self-determination as a nation, that as a nation Afrikaners should have their own government and land that they would inhabit more or less exclusively to themselves. The proposed Afrikaner homeland would incorporate parts of the northwestern Cape, southern Namibia, including parts of the Karoo and the Kalahari and Namib deserts (Race Relations Survey, 1988/8 p. 645). This demand pointed to possible future political negotiations with strong race, ethnic, and class overtones.

The notion of the Afrikaner intransigence and ideological unity however has not been quite true. Over the years the Afrikaner population class structure has become more differentiated, including rural agricultural workers, the unskilled working class, and urban professionals. Consequently, over time, the politics of the Afrikaner population have changed. In the middle of the 1980s Afrikaner politics distinctly changed and appeared class based, with the rural population favoring separate development along race lines, and the urban and professional population favoring some power-sharing with blacks (Baker, 1985).

Other Whites

As mentioned in chapter 1, of the 4.7 million whites, Afrikaners make up 3.3 million, with the rest comprising the English, the Portuguese, Italians, whites of Jewish descent, and other groups. The non-Afrikaner white groups played a major role in the running of the economy and their political support crucial in maintaining the system of separate development. The possibility of them abandoning ship was thus seen as a big factor in determining the future of South Africa. At the same time a number of them were involved in the anti-apartheid struggle ("South Africa Now," 1990[1]). In a study conducted in 1986, 45 percent of South African whites told the London Times that they were unhappy with apartheid, and 30 percent said they would accept the concept of one person, one vote (Minter, 1987). While these statistics were not large, they reflected dissension within the white population. While the white population could not be described as polarized, however, some level of dissension over the future of the country and the role of blacks could be discerned. Furthermore, young white males, (estimated at 7,000 in 1985), including Afrikaners were refusing to respond to draft call-ups (Baker; 1985). As years of apartheid progressed, so did the numbers of draft call-up dissenters increase, resulting in a new category of refugees living abroad, and waiting for the apartheid system to be eradicated, or collapse.

White Emigration

Continued unrest in South Africa, combined with economic pressure resulting from the withdrawal of overseas investment prompted emigration of the white population. In June 1986 the London Times reported a three-fold increase compared to previous years in the number of British passport holders coming from South Africa to take up permanent residence in Britain. Australia also saw a sharp increase. The number of South African nationals migrating to Australia increased fourfold in 1985-6 compared to 1984-5 (Trainor, 1990). New Zealand also experienced a significant increase of South African immigrants around this period of years. These came either directly from South Africa, or from a second country like Australia (Trainor, 1990). In 1991 a Market Research Africa study predicted that about 250,000 of South Africa's five million whites would migrate over the next five years because of political and economic instability. Emigration trends were cited as growing particularly among those aged 16 to 24 (Wall Street Journal, 1991).

The emigration trends described above were important in that they reduced quite significantly, the political and economic power base of the Nationalist government. Not only was that a loss of potential supporters for racist political ideology, it was also a loss of some of the crucial skills that the black majority still had to acquire. In short, as far as the white population was concerned, both positive and negative indicators for future political dynamics could be discerned. On the one hand there was indication that a significant number of whites favored some form of power sharing with blacks. This was a positive sign for all South Africans. Also, the gradual increase in out-migration of some segments of the white population eroded the ruling Afrikaner's power-base, thus a positive for the black population.

BLACK POLITICAL ORGANIZATIONS

While the existence of the black-white dichotomy was taken for granted in the South African political arena, an examination of the dynamics within the black population revealed that apartheid stimulated, and produced a divided society. A new government that transcended societal divisions thus appeared crucial. As the country entered the 1990s a number of political movements were on the scene, and contended for power in a new South African democracy. Among the "major" national movements were: the African National Congress (ANC), the Pan Africanist Congress (PAC, the Azania People's Organization (AZAPO), the Black Consciousness Movement (BCM), the United Democratic Front (UDF),[2] the Mass Democratic Movement (MDM), the South African Communist Party (SACP), and others.

The above named organizations gave some general indication of their preferences for the socio-political arrangements of a new South African society. However, none of them had concrete ideas on the sort of constitution that would work best for a new South Africa. On the one hand the ANC, which was closer to the UDF and the MDM's position than that of the PAC, envisioned a non-racial democratic transformation of South Africa in which no racial group dominated another. On the other, there was a desire to see a society in which all people, black and white, lived as equals in peace. The ANC released a document that set out its vision for a future South Africa. The document, entitled "Constitutional Guidelines for a Democratic South Africa," proposed the following:

- a multiparty democracy in a unitary state
- universal suffrage based on the principle of one person one vote
- a bill of rights that would be enforceable by an independent judiciary
- the protection of cultural language and language rights, freedom of association, the press and religion
- independent trade unions; land redistribution coupled with recognition of private property rights
- a ban on all forms of racism and tribalism
- a mixed economy; and

- declared South Africa to be a non-aligned state committed to the principles of the charter of the Organization of African Unity (OAU) and the charter of the United Nations (Sechaba, 1989).

PAC, AZAPO, and BCM

These organizations, closer to each other ideologically than they were to the ANC, articulated a South Africa in Africanist terms, which was to be free of white minority domination. Fundamentally, the difference between the PAC and the ANC in particular, could be pointed to their conflicting responses to the question "Who owns the land?" Their point of departure was, and remains on the language of the Freedom Charter adopted by the ANC in 1959, purporting that "South Africa belongs to all who live in it, black and white." This phrase became controversial and led to some members leaving the ANC to start the PAC. The PAC vehemently opposed, and still opposes the language of the Freedom Charter. The PAC argued that by proclaiming that South Africa belongs to all who live in it, the ANC was denying a historical fact and reality that South Africa belonged to the indigenous people of South Africa, and that their land was auctioned for sale to all who live in it. The PAC emphasized its commitment to overthrowing the white minority government, and its domination, and the restoration of the land to its rightful owners, who are African. The PAC's sentiment on African land ownership is expressed in its maxim that reads, "Izwe Elethu" meaning "The Land is Ours" (The PAC Manifesto Abridged, 1962).

Furthermore, the PAC was opposed to the ANC's alliance with the South African Communist Party (SACP) that incorporated members of the white group. This alliance, the PAC argued, constituted an ungodly sacrifice of the African material interests as it was an alliance of master (former or current) and slave, the exploiter and exploited, the oppressor and the oppressed, because all the white allies were bourgeoisie and could only be interested in maintaining the status which served their interests (Sobukwe, 1962). The PAC asserted that it was the African, who was both indigenous to South Africa and constituted its majority, to determine the future course of the country (Motlhabi, 1984). Interestingly it was not only the PAC that opposed the ANCs alliance with the SACP, some western governments (the U.S., Britain, and West Germany to name a few), and groups opposed this alliance, for reasons different from the PAC.

The PACs position thus put an emphasis on birthright and equality rather than race and equality. Unless blacks and whites cooperated as humans, and not as race categories, from an equal material base, and on equal terms, there could not be true cooperation between the two groups, the PAC asserted, but collaboration by blacks in their own oppression. As regards the other groups, the PAC defined "Coloreds" as Africans. Indians were regarded as possible allies if they identified with the interests of the African, and such allies were distinguished from the opportunistic merchant class (Motlhabi, 1984). Overall, the ideology of the PAC was that anyone who subscribed to majority rule, which was African rule, and paid full loyalty to Africa, would be regarded as an African.

It can be argued that the above PAC position put this organization at loggerheads with the Afrikaner Nationalist government that itself accentuated Afrikaner nationalism and opposed or felt threatened by African nationalism. Also, it was unclear how many "Coloreds," Indians, and even whites would be willing to identify with African interests and pledge loyalty to Africa. The perception, from these non-African groups was that they were being called to deemphasize some of their real cultural heritage and family genealogy that were rooted outside of South Africa. This perception had validity since while it may be possible to pledge loyalty to Africa, there is one's ancestry that cannot be denied which is part of one's basic identity. In Kenya, for instance, Indians defined themselves as Kenyans, but not African, and more specifically as Kenyan Indians.[3] Such self-identifications by individuals with a dual heritage and whose ancestry could be traced directly, and outside of South Africa seemed logical.

The preceding discussion on political organizations clearly indicated that differences over the polity of the future South Africa would be lively, and that differences in political ideologies[4] could reasonably be expected to be a source of conflict.

Inkatha

Also worth noting is the existence of KwaZulu homeland leader Chief Gatsha Buthelezi's Inkatha Freedom Party. While ideologically Inkatha was opposed to the Afrikaner Nationalist government, in particular it's racist ideology, it's position on the sanctions issue brought it closer to that government. Consequently, Inkatha was opposed by most black political organizations, in particular the UDF and its ally the ANC. Over the years conflict between the ANC and Inkatha took center stage and intensified. In an attempt to put this conflict in proper perspective and also to understand its origins and dynamics, a more extended discussion is given in the following pages. In this discussion the conflict between Inkatha and the UDF is treated as that between Inkatha and the ANC. This is so because the UDF, was founded seemingly as a proxy of the ANC, and in reality filled the vacuum after most black political organizations had been banned. Soon after the ANC and other political parties were legalized, the UDF disbanded.

Inkatha ka Zulu was founded in 1928 by King Solomon kaDinuzulu as a cultural movement aimed at preserving Zulu heritage and thus offsetting the estranging effects of western cultural patterns (Leatt, et al., 1986). It was revived in 1975 as Inkatha Yenkululeko Yesizwe, the National Cultural Liberation Movement by Chief Gatsha Buthelezi. While Inkatha originally was committed to preserving the Zulu heritage and cultural identification, its objectives shifted towards black liberation within the wider context of South Africa. As a result, its name evolved to that of Inkatha Freedom Party in attempt to embrace members from various ethnic and racial groups who were interested in the liberation of oppressed black groups. However, despite attempts at reaching out to all black South Africans, Inkatha could not shed its ethnic character. It drew most of its membership from the Zulu ethnic group. Over the years Inkatha membership got identified as not only predominantly Zulu, but also rural. One of the major goals of the Inkatha movement was the overthrow of apartheid through peaceful means (Race Relations Survey, 1988/89). Buthelezi thus criticized the government and claimed to stand for a united South Africa, with one, democratically elected government representing all the country's inhabitants (Motlhabi, 1984). Even though the expressed goal of Inkatha sounded meritorious, its leader, Buthelezi suffered heavy criticism from most blacks and black political organizations. As an appointed homeland leader (although a non-independent homeland), he was perceived as one of the individuals who collaborated with the apartheid South African government in a scheme meant to disenfranchise Africans in their own land. According to the BCM leader, Steve Biko, for instance, Buthelezi said the right things most of the time, but did so on the wrong platform (Biko, 1978), meaning that he operated within the oppressive government structures and thus remained a puppet of that government.

In his own defense, Buthelezi argued that his leadership of KwaZulu did not make him a puppet of the government, that the strategy he followed was one of many ways of fighting the apartheid government, and that he actually prevented the government from forcing KwaZulu from being a nominally independent homeland, thus allowing KwaZulu to remain an integral part of South Africa.

> If Zulus, who are the largest ethnic group in the country, had accepted independence, apartheid would have triumphed. I saved not only the birthright of Zulus but of many black people, Chief Buthelezi argued (Wren, April 18, 1990 p. A6).

Resentment against Buthelezi, however, never stopped. Young Africans expressed such resentment as early as 1978 when he was physically manhandled at the PAC leader, Mangaliso Sobukwe's funeral. Further trouble continued when several students were killed by Inkatha fighters at the

University of Zululand for allegedly showing disrespect towards them and their leader Buthelezi. In the 1990s conflict between Inkatha, the UDF and the ANC became central.

ANC VS. INKATHA FREEDOM PARTY

Differences between Inkatha, and the ANC were key in several areas. Buthelezi opposed the use of international economic sanctions and guerilla warfare as effective weapons against apartheid, as espoused by the ANC. The former, he argued, left the most downtrodden people, particularly the rural and uneducated Africans, without jobs and destitute. On the latter, he argued that guerilla warfare resulted in a culture of violence because of the ANC's call to "make black townships ungovernable." Furthermore, Buthelezi supported a free market economy for South Africa, arguing that was the only economic system that created jobs. The ANC espoused a mixed economic system and hoped to nationalize some of the country's major industries.

In some of the media, differences between the two groups were reduced to, and explained in ethnic terms, even as some Zulu members supported the Inkatha position, while other Zulu members supported the UDF/ANC position. Differences on the sanctions issue played out in the work places where two trade unions were at loggerheads. The United Workers Union Of South Africa (UWUSA), an Inkatha affiliate opposed sanctions, whilst the Congress of South African Trade Unions (COSATU), an ANC affiliate supported sanctions against South Africa. The struggles between Inkatha and the ANC, UWUSA and COSATU grew fiercer and fiercer, culminating in thousands of deaths and displacements of people from their homes. The Inkatha, ANC differences described above, unfortunately, escalated and travelled to industrial areas and other provinces, in particular where there were migrant workers.

Because Inkatha was predominantly Zulu, and the ANC leadership predominantly Xhosa, the Inkatha ANC conflict manifested itself as a Zulu-Xhosa conflict. It is worth noting that despite the political and economic differences that Inkatha and the ANC had, their respective leaders kept dialogue and communication between themselves open. The fighting that took place between Inkatha and ANC leadership was mostly one of words. Mandela and Buthelezi for instance, after a period of delay, met to discuss their differences and the violence between their followers. Also, despite ideological differences, the two men showed mutual respect for each other.[5] The physical fighting was waged, and continued to be waged by the poor, illiterate and jobless.

Several observers of the conflict described above argued that politics appeared to be dimly comprehended by the individuals involved in the fighting, and that such combatants visibly were casualties of apartheid—poor, uneducated, and jobless. A study conducted by the University of Natal researchers (of political attitudes among the fighters, comprising mostly of the youth gangs), found that only about 4 percent of those claiming allegiance to the United Democratic Front could identify its policies and leaders. Among Inkatha supporters, the figure was 16 percent (Wren, 1990). People engaged in the violence did not know what they were fighting for. This condition prompted a statement from the ANC leadership placing the blame for the prevailing violence on apartheid, and pointing to the fact that when people had been oppressed for so long, living in squalor, and single-sex hostels without their families, they became very short-tempered and prone to violence (Hani, 1991).

Placing the blame on apartheid brought the role of the state and the police in the conflict, a role already alluded to in the preceding discussion. Since the onset of the violence, the South African police had been accused of providing ammunition and support to Inkatha members. In July of 1991 it was finally uncovered that the South African government gave the Inkatha Freedom Party a sum amounting to $100,000, ostensibly to promulgate its opposition to sanctions. This revelation discredited the De Klerk apartheid government as a party that could not be trusted to engage in good faith negotiations about power sharing with blacks. Quite clearly, the government had a stake in encouraging divisions within the black population. Facing a black population divided between Inkatha and the ANC weakened the strength of the black majority. Conversely, a divided majority posed less political and economic threat to a minority group that was interested in maintaining its position of power.

In short, the Inkatha vs. UDF/ANC conflict emanated from political and economic ideological differences. However, in the process, ethnic and class distinctions could be discerned. Inkatha was perceived as highly representative of the rural, and, predominantly uneducated Zulu population group. The UDF/ANC on the other hand was perceived as highly representative of the semi-literate, literate, urban blacks, including 'Coloreds' and Indians. Differences between Inkatha and the ANC were most marked in urban areas and transcended ideological boundaries becoming a conflict between Zulu and Xhosa. Whilst this conflict was already in existence, the pressing issue was whether it would continue into the new South Africa.

SUMMARY

In overall summary, at this point in the country's history, divergent political ideologies appeared to loom large, and were potentially problematic for a future South Africa. Ideological differences in turn found expression, or manifested themselves distinctly and primarily in race, followed by ethnic identities. In other words, race and ethnic distinctions got politicized. More specifically there were white political parties and black political movements. Also, political parties like the Nationalist Party, the Conservative Party, and Inkatha had ethnic overtones, i.e. Afrikaner and Zulu. Class identities on the other appeared diffused.

The ruling Afrikaner Nationalist Party was willing to enter into negotiations with the black leadership, notably the ANC which expressed an all-embracing sentiment, and a conciliatory tone towards whites. Concurrently however, the Nationalist Party also gave covert support to Inkatha Freedom Party that opposed the ANC. At the pre-negotiation stage a question raised was who would be invited to participate at the negotiation table. Parties as divergent as the PAC, Inkatha, the Conservative Party, the church leaders and homeland leaders were cited. The actual electoral stage was another phase that South Africa had to go through, and which was expected to bring its own challenges. If the ANC won, the resilience of an ANC government against opposition from all quarters still needed to be tested and proven. In the following segment, issues perceived by South Africans as areas of concern, and which were foreseen as potentially problematic in a future South Africa are discussed, and presented in more concrete terms.

AREAS OF CONCERN IN A FUTURE SOUTH AFRICA

In January and February of 1990 preliminary interviews were conducted with a few members of the DSA group. The author made certain that members from each racial/ethnic category of the DSA group were represented. At this point, the respondents were treated more as discussants in the study than as subjects. This strategy it was believed, helped create a relaxed, open, and honest discussion on South Africa. Also, the fact that such interviews were taking place at a period when the shaping of a new South Africa was entering a new phase with the release of ANC leader Nelson Mandela, helped generate impassioned discussions.

During the interviews open-ended questions were asked. The aim was to determine what South Africans thought about post-apartheid South Africa, given the prevailing race, status, ethnicity, and class divisions. Several general points emerged from the discussions. These are presented below.

First, the general expectation was that conflict would occur after apartheid was dismantled. However, the thinking was that this conflict would not be physical aggression in the form of open warfare, or civil war. It was expected that this conflict would arise primarily from differences in political orientations. White South Africans as a group, it was felt, would not be targets of aggression from black South Africans. Blacks were described as forgiving people, who were also tired of living and witnessing violence from the state, and from their own members. There was, however, some cautionary note that prevailing social conditions could possibly create an atmosphere of tension, particularly if blacks perceived that their past disadvantaged conditions were not being fairly addressed and redressed.

Conflict was expected, although of a limited nature between the various ethnicities and races within the DSA group. However, there was indication that these groups had been insulated from one another for a number of decades and, therefore, did not know much about one another beyond the prevailing stereotypes. It was mentioned that grassroots level organizations had started, which were working at addressing historical differences. The University of Western Cape, for instance, which because of apartheid laws had been for "Coloreds" only, had not only opened doors to the other race groups, but students were also involved in groups that were working at addressing issues that could cause and exacerbate conflict. The aim of these student groups was to transmit this outlook to the rest of society.

Conflict between the ANC and UDF in one camp, and Inkatha in the other, was expected to continue. However, this conflict was not expected to escalate to the rest of South Africa. This conflict was seen as an issue between the ANC/UDF, and Inkatha rank and file. Also, such conflict was perceived as emanating from socio-economic factors rather than divergent political ideology per se.

A common theme was that homeland leaders would have to be invited to participate in the new political dispensation otherwise some would resist any new democratic process that threatened their established authority. The issue of the homeland policy and homeland leaders was seen as a challenge and thus presented a potential source of conflict that would need to be addressed and resolved. Generally, it was felt that people who had been forcefully removed from their original areas, legally should be allowed to return to those areas. Also, official borders that formed lines of demarcation would have to be removed.

The black middle-class was a source of concern because of its ambiguous position. As a result, the black middle-class was perceived as a group that could shift alliances between whatever ruling class, and the majority of the oppressed people. At the same time the role of the black middle-class was recognized particularly in moving some of the economic power from whites to blacks.

The role of trade unions was seen as crucial in the running of the South African economy. In a future South Africa a trade union movement was expected to act as a political "watch dog" critical of any government policies perceived as having an adverse impact on the interests of the workers.

There was a divergence of opinion on the kind of political dispensation South Africa would have after liberation. One view supported the notion of the recognition, and protection of minority rights. The opposite view supported the notion of one person, one vote, in a unitary state. The redistribution of land appeared crucial. How it would be carried out was seen as the biggest challenge. One suggestion was that whites owned most of the land, would have to be given incentives to sell some of that land to the government, which in turn would sell it at subsidized rates, or give to the most needy/oppressed people.

Finally, revamping the schooling system and removing inferior education was cited as important. It was recognized that a good education would prepare future South Africans, black and white, in acquiring skills necessary for running the country's economy efficiently and effectively.

RESEARCH QUESTIONS

A review of the literature on the conditions that stimulate transitional and post-independence conflict, and the conversations the author had with South Africans, resulted in the following broad questions being raised. These questions became central in providing guidance to the study published in 1994.

1. In a new South Africa, was conflict expected based on political an economic ideologies?
2. Were whites likely to be targets of hostility from blacks?
3. Was conflict likely to surface within and among the historically disadvantaged groups? If so, what would be the basis of this conflict?
4. Was conflict expected between the citizenry and homeland leaders? Between the homeland leaders and the democratically elected central government?
5. In the event of a confrontation with, or an uprising against the ruling government, could the disadvantaged group rely on the black middle-class for political alliance?

In the next chapter the research methodology used in gathering data addressing the questions raised above is presented and discussed.

NOTES

1. "South Africa Now" was a television documentary that ran under the auspice of Global Vision, NY and broadcasted in selected U.S. cities through Public Broadcasting Services (PBS) network. It's broadcasting was pro ANC.

2. In March of 1991, the United Democratic Front was disbanded. The reasons cited for this action were that the organization did not wish to compete with the ANC. Also, some of the issues that the UDF had fought for in the past had been met, or were in the process of being met. These issues included demands to have all black political organizations to be unbanned, the release of all political prisoners, and the return of political exiles. (South Africa Now. A Public Television Broadcasting).

3. This information was shared by a Kenyan national in conversation with South African Students at a South African Orientation Program in Denison University, Granville, Ohio, July-August, 1990.

4. Ideology has several different meanings for different people. As a result, its reality can be quite elusive. Taken in its colloquial sense, ideology reflects a set of assumptions, patterns of thought, specific value-system and norms that individuals, groups, and sections of society have. Simply put, ideologies reflect societal groups' mind-sets. They are worldviews that in turn are informed by people's class origin. Marx understood ideology as "false consciousness." He described ideology as "false" because of the unconsciousness of people of its real function, namely that of legitimatizing and sanctioning existing relationships of production. Marx described ideology as a phantom, a half-truth presented as total truth, its ultimate aim being to justify and legitimatize the ideas and interests of the dominant group as benefiting the whole society. To the writer's mind, all political organizations have some level of "false consciousness" which is probably why they invoke conflict between various groups.

5. The relationship between Mandela and Buthelezi dates years back when they attended Fort Hare University College together. Allegedly, Buthelezi had been a member of the ANC Youth League, but subsequently took a route different from Mandela's. Inkatha claimed paid up membership of 2.2 million. By comparison, the ANC claimed 700,000 members. However, political surveys indicated Inkatha with seldom more than 3 or 4 percent of urban black support. Inkatha also had a scattering of support from whites who preferred it's pro-market economy disposition, rather than the ANC's socialist overtones (Wren, August 3, 1991).

Chapter Four

Research Methodology

To reiterate, this chapter describes the research methodology used in the 1994 study and publication. The discussion begins with a description of the population and sample used. Next is a description of how the data were collected. Finally, a critique of the research method is presented.

DEFINING THE POPULATION

The target population for this study was identified and defined as historically disadvantaged South Africans currently studying or living in North America. This population was chosen for several reasons. First, since these individuals were outside of South Africa, it was expected that they would be in a better position to express their thoughts with minimum political and/or cultural constraints and inhibitions. Second, these individuals were studying abroad and acquiring education and experience that would be invaluable contributors in the creation of a new society. In other words, the expectation was that when they returned to South Africa, they would occupy crucial and significant positions of leadership in the implementation of new policies, and in the running of the country's economy. Their views were thus important since they were a representation of the kind of thought processes and behavioral patterns that could be expected of societal members in a new South Africa. Two United States organizations featured prominently in sponsoring disadvantaged South Africans for study in North American colleges and universities. The major sponsor was the Institute of International Education (IIE) based at the United Nations Plaza in New York City, and a black consultancy group Aurora Associates, based in Washington D.C. Beginning in 1979 a total of 1,038 South Africans had an opportunity to study abroad through the auspices of these organizations. Table 3.1 shows a summary of their demographic characteristics. The table was prepared from a report written by the Educational Opportunities Council based in Johannesburg that was the recruiting agency in South Africa. The table reflects members by gender, field of study, and racial background. Also worth mentioning are the origins in South Africa of the population members. 42 percent came from Transvaal, now called Gauteng, which is the province where the majority of black South Africans live. The province with the second largest representation is the Cape Province, now comprising the Eastern and Western Cape, with about 26 percent of the participants originating from there. In the third place Natal, now called KwaZulu-Natal, with an approximate 24 percent representation, and finally the Orange Free State with approximately a 4 percent representation (Equal Opportunity Council Report, p.6, 1990).

SAMPLE DESIGN

Owing to the exploratory nature of the study, a judgement sampling was followed in the selection of respondents. A judgement design is described a selected subgroup of the population which, on the basis of available information is judged as representative of the target population (Davis, Cosenza; 1988).

Two strategies were utilized to reach the respondents. During the years of study in the US, the author had been involved in running an orientation program for newly arriving South African students. This program ran every summer, from mid-July through end of August, at Denison University, Granville Ohio, under the auspices of both IIE and Aurora Associates.

In the course of each of these orientations a list of names and addresses of the participants was generated. Over the years a total of approximately 200 was, therefore, available to the author covering participants in the orientation program for the period 1985–1989. It should be noted that since the orientation program participants generated the list voluntarily as a mechanism for social networking while in the US, not all program participants were included. There were individuals who chose not to submit their names and forwarding addresses. To augment the above list of names, the author resorted to an informal network of South Africans in North America. A number of South Africans known to the author on a social networking basis were either studying or residing in North America. These include individuals sponsored by other agencies and institutions such as the Fulbright-Hayes Scholarship, Ford Foundation, African-American Institute, Bishop Tutu Fund, Phelp-Stokes Foundation, the United Nations Education and Training Program for Southern A (UNETPSA), and private and public university.

Table 4.1. Participants in the South African Education Program

Category	Number
Gender	
Female	102
Male	210
Field of Study/Expertise	
Bachelors	159
Masters	139
Ph.D.	14
Business	39
Education	69
Engineering	51
Health Science	19
Law	6
Psychology	12
Natural Science	66
Social Science	44
Urban Planning & Architecture	5
Racial Group	
Africans	236
Mixed Race	47
Indians	29

Source: Figures used above (excluding racial background), are primarily from "The training of disadvantaged black South Africans in the United States of America: An analysis the academic and occupational achievement of former South African Education program participants." Educational Opportunities Council SAEP/SAHEP participants report statistics for 1979–1990.

Altogether, approximately 250 names and addresses were secured. A questionnaire (see Appendix D) was then mailed or given to these individuals. In short, the lists of names generated at the Denison University orientation program, individuals known to the writer on a social networking basis became the population sample.

PILOT TESTING

In June of 1990 the questionnaire was pilot-tested on 20 South Africans belonging to the DSA group and residing in the New England area. According to Sheatsley (1983) pilot testing can range anywhere from a half dozen cases done locally, to 100 cases or more conducted in several different localities to determine differences in responses towards similar test items. Also, according to Sheatsley it takes no more than 12–25 cases to reveal major difficulties and weaknesses in a pilot tested questionnaire. Sheatsley's position supports Sudman's argument that a pilot sample of 20–50 cases is usually sufficient to discover major flaws in questionnaires before they damage the main study.

Researchers are divided on the issue of how closely the pilot study subjects should resemble the actual respondents of the study. Some have suggested that the pretest subjects be as similar as possible to the target population (Tull and Hawkins, 1976; Zaltman and Burger, 1969), whilst others have argued that this precaution is not always necessary (Galtung, 1969; Brown and Beik, 1969). The author however, preferred to have the pilot test subjects resemble the target population as closely as possible, particularly because it was a special and unique one.

The pilot test proved helpful. Some questions needed rewording for clarification. Also, some terms often taken for granted by sociologists needed more simplification for better interpretation by non-sociologists.

DISTRIBUTION PROCEDURE

A total of 200 questionnaires with a cover letter were mailed out in July, of 1990. A further 120 questionnaires were taken to the 1990 Denison University South African Student summer orientation program. These were distributed to the newly arrived South African orientation program participants. In December 1990 the author also had an opportunity of attending the IIE sponsored winter conference of South Africans, mainly students, at the University of Maryland, in College Park. Additional questionnaires were distributed at this conference. Finally, during the month of January 1991, additional questionnaires were mailed to non-respondents with a cover letter reminding them to respond.

CRITIQUE OF THE RESEARCH METHOD

The issues raised from the research method center around the inaccessibility of the target population, sample self-selection, sample size, and the extent of generalizability of the research findings.

The major problem of the study was the elusiveness of the target population. Because of the policy of confidentiality the author could not gain access to an official listing of all South Africans of the DSA group. She therefore relied on a judgement sample design based on a list generated on a voluntary basis. This problem resulted in the reduction of the attainable sample size. Generalizations from a small sample to the targeted population could therefore, not be easily made.

One of the major weaknesses of judgement samples is that variability and bias estimates cannot be measured or controlled. Another potential weakness associated with judgement samples is that they often require strong assumptions or considerable knowledge of the target population and the selected subgroup (Davis and Cosenza, 1988). This author was, however, familiar enough with the SA sample. She was a member of that group. She also had a chance of residing the respondents for 3–4 weeks during the summer orientations.

Since the author added to the list individuals that she knew on a social networking basis, the sample could have been self-selective. This element, however, was viewed as a strength in the study rather than a weakness in that the sample could comprise individuals who responded because they viewed research projects as important, and who viewed this particular study as both important and needed. In point of fact, this sentiment was expressed repeatedly to the author in inform conversations. This notwithstanding having respondents who were self selected, might have introduced a systematic bias to the sample.

As already indicated, participants in the study belonged to a special and unique population. They were a select group of individuals acquiring education outside of South Africa. Whilst special populations are frequently chosen for analysis, generally the attainable sample size is always small since much more effort must be expended to locate them and to obtain cooperation (Sudman, 1983). In this study the target population was not only difficult to locate, it was also not clustered in one area, instead members were dispersed throughout North America. Mailing out questionnaires was thus the best way to reach individual members. Some questionnaires were not returned despite written and telephone reminders. Cooperation in most research is always a problem, and in this study a similar problem was experienced.

Finally, as already mentioned, the study was based on the views of DSAs North America. These individuals were not necessarily a highly representative sample of the cross section of the population of DSA on the ground in South Africa. This warranted extra caution in generalizing the results.

To sum up, in this chapter the research methodology was discussed, the demographics of the population from which the sample was drawn were outlined, the research procedures were explained, and a critique provided. In the following chapters five and six the results of the data analysis are presented.

Chapter Five

Data Presentation and Analysis
Part I

In this chapter, the response rate as well as the demographics of the respondents in the 1994 study and publication are discussed. This is followed by a quantitative and qualitative analysis of the data. The chapter concludes with a summary of some of the findings of the study.

RESPONSE RATE

As mentioned in the preceding chapter, approximately 250 questionnaires were mailed or handed out to prospective respondents. Altogether, a total of 130 completed questionnaires were returned, yielding a response rate of 52 percent. Of these, three were unusable. The author therefore ended up with 127 completed, usable questionnaires. This author felt comfortable with this response rate since the topics covered in the questionnaire were regarded by some members of the DSA as sensitive and delicate. In fact, the author was made aware of the fact that some potential respondents did not feel comfortable giving their response on some of the items included in the questionnaire. This response is typical among the historically disadvantaged groups who have suffered various forms of oppression. They develop distrust and a perception that "surveys" and "research" are another tool that is used for their own oppression (Miller 1975). Despite assurance of confidentiality, some potential respondents, in conversation with the author, expressed reservations that their responses on the questionnaire could be traced back to them, and at a later stage, used in a manner that would be harmful to them.

Table 5.1 summarizes the demographic characteristics of the respondents. In general, a majority of the respondents were male (64 percent); in their twenties (54 percent); in the social sciences, education, and business (60 percent); most from the then Transvaal area (44 percent); a large majority are African (85 percent).

ANALYSIS OF DATA

Generally, the questionnaire was designed to draw out the respondents' views on the following areas: political and economic ideologies, possible reactions of blacks towards whites after apartheid, reactions of blacks towards each other, reactions towards homelands and their leaders, and the black middle-class.

Responses from each section of the questionnaire were grouped into low and high categories by first combining 1s (strongly disagree) with 2s (disagree); and then the 4s (agree) with 5s (strongly agree). The end product of this recoding was a set of responses represented by three broad categories, which were 1 for "disagree," 2 for "don't know"; and 3 for "agree." The reason for this regrouping was to increase the number of cases in each table cell. An earlier run, for example, produced tables where only a few cases were recorded in either "strongly agree" or "agree" categories. It, was therefore, more expedient to combine the two categories into one "agree" or "disagree" category.

The "don't know" responses were left as a separate and distinct category rather than combining them with either the "disagree" or "agree" categories. This was done deliberately for a number of reasons. Research on the treatment of "don't know" indicates that this category makes for a useful, educational, and interesting analysis. Ferber (1966), provided evidence suggesting non-randomness of the "don't know" category.

He demonstrated that item nonresponse is systematically related to such variables as sex, age, and educational level. Poe, et al. (1988), argued that respondents might legitimately not know an answer because they do not have the information, have never thought about the issue, or have not formulated a position or point of view

On the other hand, Bishop, et al. (1986) argued that people do have an opinion to offer even on fictitious, or difficult matters, the willingness to express one's view depending on one's educational background. Whatever the debate is on the meaning of "don't know," it should be recognized that with certain issues it does not make much sense for many individuals not to have an opinion, particularly on topical matters.

In the social sciences, it is axiomatic that attitudes, views, and perceptions, are very much informed by people's background, in other words, by people's personal experiences, and who they are. For this reason some of the demographic variables were seen as important and used as independent variables:

Table 5.1. Demographic Characteristics of the Respondents

Characteristics	Number	Percent
Gender: Female	46	35.7
Male	81	64.3
Age: Less than 21	9	7.3
21-30	67	53.7
31-40	35	28.5
41 and above	13	10.6
Field of Study/Expertise		
Engineering	18	14.3
Social Science	28	22.2
Business	22	17.5
Natural Science	13	10.3
Education	27	21.4
Health	8	5.6
*Other	11	8.7
Province of origin		
Cape	33	26.0
Natal	31	24.6
Transvaal	56	43.7
Orange Free State	7	5.6
Ethnic group		
Mixed-Race	11	8.7
Indian	8	6.3
**Sovenga	52	40.9
Xhosa	21	16.5
Zulu	35	27.6
Duration of stay abroad		
Less than a year	53	41.3
1 to 5 years	54	42.9
6 years and over	20	15.7

*Other includes the following categories: Animal Science
Biological Sciences
City Planning,
Communications
Journalism, and Law
**Sotho, Venda, Shangaan.

age, gender, ethnic background (ETHGROUP), and duration of stay in a specific area, in this instance away from South Africa (DURES). Ethnic background was, for the most part treated as the major variable because ethnicity appeared to play a role in the South African political scene, thus reflecting a potential problem for South Africa in the future. The author was therefore curious to find out if there would be differences in the responses given by the respondents on the various questionnaire items based on ethnic background.

The dependent variables included item 16, capitalist/free enterprise economic system (CAPEC), through item 70, Africans versus the disadvantaged people (AFRIDIS) on the questionnaire. (See appendix C for the listing of item acronyms). The quantitative data from the questionnaire were analyzed on the SPSS-X program found in the Cyber mainframe computer of the University of Massachusetts at Amherst. Means, cross tabulations, and chi-square tests were the primary statistical tools used to explore the questions raised at the end of Chapter 3. The results of the quantitative analysis are reported and discussed below.

FINDINGS

Conflict Based On Political and Economic Ideological Differences

To address the first research question, a cross tabulation was run between ethnic group (ETHGROUP), the various political organizations (ANC UDF), and the various economic systems (CAPEC through COMEC). The cross tabulation on political organizations revealed some interesting results. Among all political movements, the ANC received the support of 68 (53.3 percent) of the respondents, the UDF received the second largest support from 65 (51.2 percent) of the respondents. The agree and disagree responses on the BCM were more or less split in the middle. 45 (35.4 percent) of the respondents disagreed that the ideology of this organization was the best for South Africa, 44 (34.6 percent) agreed with its ideology. Another 38 (30.2 percent) respondents did not know. Regarding the PAC, 55 (43.3 percent) of the respondents disagreed with the ideology of this organization, 36 (28.3 percent) did not know, and 36 (28.3 percent) agreed (See Table 5.2).

A further scrutiny of the responses revealed the following results: of the Mixed-race group supported the UDF, followed by the ANC. Specifically 63.6 percent of this group supported the UDF, and 54.5 percent supported ANC. Members of the Indian group supported the ANC—75 percent—followed the UDF—50 percent. It is worth noting that both the Mixed-race group and the Indian group disagreed in large numbers with the ideology of both the BCM and PAC. Specifically, 54.5 percent of the Mixed-race group disagreed with the BCM and 45.5 percent disagreed with the PAC. Regarding the Indian group, 62.5 percent disagreed with both political movements. Low support of the BCM among the Mixed-race group and Indian group is a curiosity considering that one of the earlier objectives of this organization was to influence group members to see themselves as part of the oppressed group.

Table 5.2. Responses: Political Ideology That Is Best for South Africa

ETHGROUP	n	ANC	UDF	BCM	PAC
Mixed-Race	(11)				
Disagree		2(18.2)	1(9.1)	6(54.5)	5(45.5)
Don't Know		3(27.3)	3(27.3)	3(27.3)	4(36.4)
Agree		6(54.5)	7(63.6)	2(18.2)	2(18.2)
Indian	(8)				
Disagree		2(25)	3(37.5)	5(62.5)	5(62.5)
Don't Know		1(12.5)			
Agree		6(75)	4(50.0)	3(37.5)	3(37.5)
***Sovenga**	(52)				
Disagree		18(34.6)	13(25)	16(30.8)	20(38.5)
Don't Know		8(15.4)	14(26.9)	16(30.8)	14(26.9)
Agree		26(50)	25(48.1)	20(38.5)	18(34.6)
Xhosa	(21)				
Disagree		8(38.1)	5(23.8)	8(38.1)	9(42.9)
Don't Know		3(14.3)	7(33.3)	5(23.8)	2(9.5)
Agree		10(47.6)	9(42.9)	8(38.1)	10(47.6)
Zulu	(35)				
Disagree		5(14.3)	6(17.1)	10(28.6)	16(45.7)
Don't Know		10(28.6)	9(25.7)	14(40)	16(45.7)
Agree		20(57.1)	20(57.1)	11(31.4)	3(8.6)
Total	(127)				
Disagree		35(27.6)	28(22)	45(35.4)	55(43.3)
Don't Know		24(18.9)	34(26.8)	38(29.9)	36(28.3)
Agree		68(53.5)	65(51.2)	44(34.6)	36(28.3)

ETHGROUP on ANC: Chi-square = 9.656; d.f.= 8; p =. 290
ETHGROUP on UDF: Chi-square = 4.244; d.f.= 8·; p= .834
ETHGROUP on BCM: Chi-square = 8.771; d.f.= 8; p=.877
ETHGROUP on PAC: Chi-square = 18.863; d.f. = 8; p= .015
ETHGROUP: ethnic group
ANC:African Nationalist Congress
UDF:United Democratic Front
BCM:Black Consciousness Movement
PAC:Pan Africanist Congress
*Sovenga: Sotho, Venda, Shangaan.

In other words, one of the aims of BCM was to influence both Mixed-race group members and Indians to define themselves as "blacks" (Biko, 1978). The response on the PAC made sense in that the sentiment expressed in its ideology emphasizes "Africanism" which, because of their ancestry, which lies outside of South Africa, either India or Europe, some members of the Mixed-race group and Indian group could not quite identify with.

Among the African groups, the ANC received the largest support followed by UDF. Responses on the BCM appeared ambiguous, particularly for the Sovenga and Xhosa groups. 30.8 percent of the Sovenga group, for instance disagreed with the BCM. The same percentage did not know, and

38.5 agreed. For the Xhosa group, responses were split, 38.1 percent disagree with the BCM and the same percentage agreed. A smaller percentage (23.8) did not know. For the Zulu group, a large percentage (40) did not know. 31.4 percent agreed, and 28. 6 percent disagreed with the BCM. The results of the quantitative analysis are reported in Table 5.2.

Whilst of the four political movements, which are the ANC, UDF, BCM, and PAC, the latter received the least support from the total respondents. What could be discerned from the results was fact that the PAC received the largest support from the Xhosa group—47.6 percent—and the least support from the Zulu group 8.6 percent. The reason for this large discrepancy in responses between the two ethnic groups could be due to the historical formation of the PAC. First, when it was banned it had been in existence only for approximately a year after having broken off from the ANC[1]. One can argue that the PAC had a relatively short life span within the country to get itself and its ideology widely known. Second, before it was banned, it was most active around the Cape Province and the Transvaal areas, specifically around the Cape Town and Johannesburg metropolitan areas rather than Natal or Orange Free State. This response suggested a possible correlation between regionalism and political party preference that is worth studying in the future.

The chi-square statistical analysis on the PAC also proved significant revealing some differences of opinion. Its value was 18.86, with 8 degrees freedom and a p value of .015 (See Table 5.2). The overall low responses by respondents on the BCM and PAC seemed logical. Generally individuals who supported the ANC, and UDF, tended not to support the BCM and PAC.

Another observation worth highlighting was that the responses indicated more clarity on political organizations that respondents were opposed to rather than those they supported. For example, government-sponsored, homeland linked political organizations, and white political parties received the least support from the respondents. (See Table 5.3). Also, there was a wide gap between the most supported, which were, the ANC and UDF, and the most opposed political organizations, being the Conservative Party through the Labor Party. The ANC and UDF, for example, drew support of 53.5 percent and 51.2 percent of the respondents respectively. Whilst this response was high in relative terms, it was not an overwhelmingly high support rate in absolute terms. This response possibly due to the fact that most black organizations had either been banned, or harassed by the state for a number of years, thus making campaigning and the recruitment of new members a challenge. During informal conversations with the researcher, some respondents indicated that they were simply not sure which political party to support. Said differently, the various black political organizations were still being scrutinized by potential supporters. Also, some members indicated in conversation with the researcher, that their support was somewhere between the ANC and the PAC, they had not quite decided which of the two organizations to support as reflected by the responses of individuals of Xhosa background in Tables 5.2 and 5.3. This response reflected the start of an alignment and realignment phase as historically disadvantaged people were being drawn into the political process for the first time in their lives.

The questionnaire items which probed the respondents' responses on which political organization they thought expressed an ideology that would work best for South Africa, invoked several written comments which indicated lively debate, and thus an area of concern. These were the comments given:

> I am of the opinion that the ideology of most of the organizations will have to undergo change for South Africa to go through a peaceful transition for liberation. Historical differences and the after effects of apartheid will make it hard for any one ideology to become accepted at a broad-based level (Respondent # 1).

Table 5.3. Support For Political Organizations By Ethnic Group Expressed in Percentages

Organization	Ethnic Group					% Total
	Mixed-Race	Indian	*Sovenga	Xhosa	Zulu	
ANC	54.5	75	50	47.6	57.1	53.5
UDF	63.6	50	48.1	42.9	57.1	51.2
BCM	18.2	37.5	38.5	38.1	31.4	34.6
PAC	18.2	37.5	34.6	47.6	8.6	28.3
**DP	9.0	12.5	15.4	14.3	28.6	18.4
***NIC	18.2	50.0	15.4	9.5	17.2	17.3
CP	9.0		7.7	4.8	8.6	7.1
LP			3.8		11.4	4.8
IFP					8.5	2.4
TC	9.0		1.9			1.6
NP	9.0		1.9			1.6
HNP				4.8		.8

Note: See Appendix B for a description of all the organizations' abbreviations. Also note that the rows and columns do not add up to 100 percent owing to the fact that respondents were allowed to show preference for more than one political organization.
* Sotho, Venda, and Shangaan.
** This response on the Democratic Party (DP), which is a liberal white political party is striking. The respondents may have confused its name with the United Democratic Front. Also, the term "democratic" generally presupposes equality and inclusiveness, concepts that are always viewed in a positive light.
*** The response on the Natal Indian Congress (NIC) appears logic. Historically, the NIC has been in alliance with the ANC.

I believe that what South Africa needs is unity. The so-called anti apartheid movements need to move towards more tolerance and open mindedness, as well as appreciation of each other and views. I don't at this point believe any one ideology is the best (Respondent # 36).

All black political organizations (excluding Inkatha) have valid points which I feel should be accommodated to a lesser or greater extent. I do not believe that any one of them is the best (Respondent # 109).

Table 5.3 presents a summary of the rate of support given each political organization, broken down by ethnic group, and expressed in percentages. The last column in Tabs is the overall support rate given for each political organization by all the respondents regardless of ethnic background, also expressed in percentage.

The majority of the respondents, however, supported the notion of a future Africa based on a one person, one vote in a unitary state. Specifically 112 (88.2 percent) of the respondents agreed with this notion, 6 (4.7 percent) disagreed, and 9 (7.1 percent) did not know. 86 (67.7 percent) disagreed with the notion of a constitution that recognized minority or group rights in a unitary state. 12 (9.4 percent) did not know, and 29 (22.8 percent) agreed. The 29 (22.8 percent) who agreed with a constitution that recognized minority or group rights included individuals from the various ethnic groups. Specifically, 4 members (36.4 percent) from the Mixed-race group agreed, 2 (25 percent) Indians agreed, 13 members (25 percent) of the Sotho, Venda, and Shangaan group agreed, 2 members (9.5 percent) from the Xhosa group agreed, and 8 members (22.8 percent) of Zulu background agreed. To the researcher's mind this response probably reflected the concern that some South Africans had over the protection of culture and language of the various racial/ethnic groups.

Generally, however, most disadvantaged South Africans are leery of a constitution that emphasizes group rights, particularly if such rights translate into racial/ethnic preferential treatment, and a continued maintenance of a privileged position by certain groups. On an abstract level, this response recognized the importance of language and culture, whilst attempting to separate or negate the importance of race. On a practical level, as mentioned in chapter 1, whether language, culture, and race can be separated is a challenge yet to be met, as in South Africa, these variables remain highly intertwined.

On the notion of a future South Africa that is based on the partitioning of the country into a confederation of states, 89 (70.1 percent) respondents disagreed, 25 (19.7 percent) did not know, and 13 (10.2 percent) agreed.

On the issue of the economic system there was also consensus among the respondents. The majority preferred a mixed economy as opposed to a capitalist and communist economy. 81 (63.8 percent) of the respondents, for example, disagreed that a capitalist economic system would work best for South Africa. 84 (66.1 percent) respondents agreed that a part-capitalist/part-socialist economic system would work best for South Africa. In response to the statement about the communist system, 93 (73.2 percent) of the respondents disagreed that this system would work best for South Africa (see Table 5.4).

A chi-square analysis of the responses on the question of which economic system would work best for South Africa revealed no significant differences of opinion among the respondents. (Also reflected in Table 5.4). The following comment offered in one of the questionnaires seemed

Table 5.4. Responses on Economic Systems

ETHGROUP	(n)	CAPEC	CAPSOC	SOCEC	COMEC
Mixed-Race	(11)				
Disagree		8(72.7)	2(18.2)	6(54.5)	9(81.8)
Don't Know			1(9.1)	3(27.3)	1(9.1)
Agree		3(27.3)	8(72.7)	2(18.2)	1(9.1)
Indian	(8)				
Disagree		6(75)	2(25)	2(25)	6(75)
Don't Know		1(12.5)	2(25)	1 (12.5)	2(25)
Agree		1(12.5)	4(50)	5(62.5)	
***Sovenga**	(52)				
Disagree		35(67.3)	7(13.5)	21(40.4)	36(69.2)
Don't Know		10(19.2)	6(11.5)	15(28.8)	11(21.2)
Agree		7(13.5)	39(75)	16(30.8)	5(9.6)
Xhosa	(21)				
Disagree		15(71.4)	6(28.6)	10(47.6)	15(71.4)
Don't Know		1(4.8)	4(19)	5(23.8)	3(14.3)
Agree		5(23.8)	11(52.4)	6(28.6)	3(14.3)
Zulu	(35)				
Disagree		17(48.6)	3(8.6)	20(57.1)	27(77.1)
Don't Know		6(17.1)	10(28.6)	8(22.9)	7(20)
Agree		12(34.3)	22(62.9)	7(20)	1(2.9)
Total	(127)				
Disagree		81(63.8)	20(15.7)	59(46.5)	93(73.2)
Don't Know		18(14.2)	23(18.1)	32(25.2)	24(18.9)
Agree		28(22)	84(66.1)	36(28.3)	10(7.9)

ETHGROUP on CAPEC; chi-square = 10.515; d.f. = 8; p. = . 230
ETHGROUP on CAPSOC; chi-square= 9.717; d.f.= 8; p. = . 285
ETHGROUP on SOCEC; chi-square= 7.785; d.f.= 8; p.= .454
ETHGROUP on COMEC; chi-square= 4.492; d.f. = 8; p. = .810
ETHGROUP: ethnic group
CAPEC: capitalist economic system CAPSOC: part capitalist,part-socialist economic system
SOCEC: socialist economic system COMEC: communist economic system
* Sotho, Venda, Shangaan.

to indicate quite succinctly why the majority of the respondents chose a mixed economy:

> I believe people, rather than ideologies should be served. People and societies by their nature are dynamic, not static. Any socio-economic system should be generally dynamic. The European ideologies of capitalism, socialism, and communism are too static. Besides, they have been designed for 19th century and early 20th century Europe. We need something designed by us, to accommodate our particular circumstances (Respondent # 109).

Preference for a mixed economy was logical. Historically, because of discriminatory laws in South Africa blacks had not felt the benefits of profit making and economic growth. Modernization theory in social theory argues that industrialization, and economic development, are usually followed by a progressive decline in racial and ethnic discrimination. This happens or should happen because of the shift from particularistic (or traditional) to universalistic (or technical) criteria for determining who gains access to social, political, and economic resources. In other words, according to the theory of modernization the expectation is that an individual's ascriptive status should not be of as much importance as his/her acquired status. Also, according to this view, economic development imposes norms of rationality and universalism on the citizenry promoting flexibility, open-mindedness, political democracy, and class fluidity (McClelland 1961; Inkeles and Smith, 1974).

Modernization theory in the South African situation was not quite applicable. Instead, at the time the country was experiencing economic growth, the social, economic, and political conditions of blacks remained poor. Whilst most members of the white population had the technical skills, and could therefore participate meaningfully in the economic sector, profit making thrived on racial discrimination, and was achieved at the expense, and availability of cheap black labor. Expressed in a somewhat different manner, whilst South Africa experienced economic growth, its racial problems were not resolved. Instead, racial particularism was the parameter within which "rational" business solutions were sought. For example, within the industries job titles for skilled African workers were changed to reflect lower status. African painters were painter assistants, remaining officially classified as unskilled labor, and thus receiving less pay Stokes and Harris, 1978). The same pattern, it can be argued, applied in professional positions as well. African managers often received "assistant to" titles or specialized in African or black affairs. They were typically assigned to non-line management, "relations" jobs, for example employee relations manager, industrial relations manager, and so on (Mangaliso, 1992). These jobs received a lower differential status, and thus less pay.

While the merits of capitalism were recognized, in that this system stimulates economic growth, to counteract its negative effects, one being that of exploitation, and to introduce social responsibility on the part of business enterprises, a combination of capitalism with socialism appeared fair. It could also argued that events which took place in Eastern Europe beginning in the late 1980s influenced the respondents against choosing pure communism and socialism as weaknesses inherent in those systems were exposed.

It is, however, worth noting that whilst 6 or 75 percent of the Indian group respondents disagreed with a capitalist economy for a future South Africa, 5 or 62.5 percent, agreed that a socialist economy was the best for South Africa. (See Table 5.4). This was an interesting response in that it belied the notion that individuals of Indian descent were linked to the business or merchant sector and would be expected, or inclined to support a capitalist economy. This response may well have been a rejection by the respondents of the prevailing belief, real or imagined, about Indian entrepreneurship, in favor of a more radical economic view. Quite possibly, the Indian respondents held radical political and economic viewpoints. Also, socialism as a way of life that has always part of the Indian community and family tradition. Emphasis is on supporting and taking care of the members of the group, sharing available resources, and respecting elders by giving them deference. This is the spirit of socialism that has made the South African Indian community appear cohesive. Furthermore, most members despite socio-economic status adhered to this way of life.

Also worth noting was the narrow gap reflected among the Zulu group between those who disagreed that a capitalist economy would work best for a future South Africa, and those who agreed. Specifically, 17 (48.6 percent) disagreed and 12 (34.3 percent) agreed. (Also Table 5.4). This response raised the question why the narrow gap? A closer scrutiny of the respondents' demographic however revealed no clear pattern. Individuals with rural and urban origins were well represented in both the disagree and agree categories. The same also applied to age, and fields of study groupings.

HOSTILITY TOWARDS WHITES

On the question of whether in a future South Africa whites were likely to be targets of hostility from blacks because of past unfair practices, a large number of respondents, 89 (70.1 percent) disagreed with the statement that blacks would seek to avenge themselves for past unfair practices suffered under apartheid laws. 19 (15 percent) did not know, and 19 (15 percent) agreed. (See Table 5.5).

Table 5.5. Responses: Hostility Towards Whites

ETHROUP	n	AVENGE	GROUPAT
Mixed-Race	(11)		
Disagree		9(81.8)	3(27.3)
Don't know		1(9)	1(9)
Agree		1(9)	7(63.6)
Indian	(8)		
Disagree		7(87.5)	2(25)
Don't Know		1(12.5)	1(12.5)
Agree			5(62.5)
***Sovenga**	(52)		
Disagree		36(69.2)	10(19.2)
Don't Know		7(13.5)	9(17.3)
Agree		9(17.3)	33(63.5)
Xhosa	(21)		
Disagree		14(66.6)	4(19)
Don't Know		3(14.3)	4(19)
Agree		4(19)	13(61.9)
Zulu	(35)		
Disagree		23(65.7)	5(14.2)
Don't know		7(20)	4(11.4)
Agree		5(14.3)	26(74.2)
Total	(127)		
Disagree		89(70.1)	24(18.9)
Don't Know		19(15)	19(15)
Agree		19(15)	84(66.1)

ETHGROUP on AVENGE; chi-square = 3.549; d.f. = 8; p. = .895
ETHGROUP on GROUPAT; chi-square = 2.457; d.f. = 8; p. = .963
ETHGROUP: ethnic group
AVENGE: blacks will seek to avenge themselves
GROUPAT: black vs. white group hostility
*Sotho, Venda, Shangaan

84 (66.1 percent) of the respondents, however, agreed with the statement that if conditions for blacks did not improve at a satisfactory pace, whites could possibly be targets of hostility. 19 (15 percent) did not know, and 24 (18.9 percent) disagreed. Again, these responses were logical. Whilst blacks would not be out to avenge themselves for past unfairness, prevailing conditions were expected to produce a sense of relative deprivation. Relative deprivation is the dissatisfaction arising from the gap between individuals' and groups' perception of the conditions they live under, compared to the conditions they believe they should have (Gurr, 1970). The sentiment of relative deprivation can contribute to alienation and foster social discontent which finds expression in collective behavior such as mass demonstrations,

rioting, insurgencies and revolutions. Such collective behavior, in particular mass demonstrations and rioting, had always been part of the South African society. In a new social order mass demonstrations and riots were expected to continue if conditions for the historically oppressed people did not improve at a satisfactory pace.

Furthermore, it is worth pointing out that 74.2 percent of the Zulu group agreed that if conditions for blacks did not improve at a satisfactory pace, whites as a group could possibly be targets of hostility. When one reviews the history of South Africa, not only was it fraught with frontier wars between blacks, specifically, Africans and whites, some of the fiercest battles took place in the Natal area.

CONFLICT AMONG THE DSA

As mentioned in chapter I conflict between blacks and whites in South Africa generally is taken as a given. Races that have been separated from one another and also existed on unequal terms cannot be expected to live in harmony, at least not overnight. Black groups have also legally been separated from each other and received differential treatment. This condition has resulted in a lack of knowledge of each group's members beyond prevailing stereotypes and some level of distrust. The researcher saw fit to include items in the questionnaire that tapped the extent of acceptance and/or knowledge of members of the various groups.

Acceptance presupposes knowledge of out group members. Such knowledge is gained through contact, particularly on a social level with members other than one's own. For this reason, the researcher included questions that asked about each group's values. To the researcher's mind, these questions could be answered with relative ease if the respondents had had contact with out group members. Interestingly, and also surprisingly, the questions in this section evoked more "don't know" responses than any other section. In other words, at this point, the number of "don't know" responses increased substantially.

Some discussion of why so many "don't know" was thus necessary.

In follow up informal interviews with some of the respondents three issues were raised about "don't knows." Firstly, some respondents indicated that they could not respond to the questions on values because they had never had an opportunity to live in close proximity with members of the other race groups, and thus did not feel qualified giving an opinion on the similarity of values. Secondly, while some respondents had contact with individual members of the other race groups, they felt uncertain about the representativeness of these individuals for their race group on the ground in South Africa. In other words, they felt that their judgment was based on limited contact and knowledge of the other race group members.

Thirdly, some members had difficulty with the questions themselves citing their lack of specificity. Values span over a number of issues, including social, political, religious economic and so on. Some respondents, for instance, indicated that intergroup and intragroup similarities and differences on a variety of values could be discerned among the different groups. On one level, it was mentioned, intergroup values were similar, and on another level different. On this issue some comments read as follows:

> Respect for life and others' comfort are shared by members from all groups (Respondent # 3).
>
> Most of the values seem to be the same, but there are a few differences, for example, religious differences.... But part of the "Coloreds," in particular Muslims, have similar religious values to Muslim Indians (Respondent # 6).

The results on the questions on similarity of values are reported in detail in Table 5.6. More respondents disagreed, specifically 64 (50.4 percent) that the values held by "Coloreds" and Indians (COLIVA) are similar. Importantly, 78 (61.4 percent) of the respondents disagreed that values held by Indians and Africans (INDAVA) are similar. 30 (23.6 percent) did not know, and 19 (15 percent) agreed.

Responses by members of the Mixed-race group were interesting. Whilst a majority of them, which was, 6 (54.5 percent) saw a similarity of values between themselves and the African group, their responses on values held by themselves and members of the Indian group were split. Specifically, 4 (36.4 percent) of the respondents agreed that values held by "Coloreds" and Indians were similar, and the same figure of 4 (36.4 percent) disagreed. Furthermore, 5 (45.5 percent) disagreed that values held by Indians and Africans were similar, 3 (27.3 percent) did not know, and the same figure agreed. Members of the Indian group, on the other hand, saw similarities in values among all groups, the largest percentage, that 6 (75 percent) being in the values held by themselves and the "Colored" group. (See Table 5.6). For the African groups, most respondents disagreed that values across racial groups were similar, except for the Xhosa group in which 10 (47 percent) agreed that values held by "Coloreds" and Indians were similar. (Also Table 5.6).

Chi-square figures produced by a cross tabulation of the independent variable ETHGROUP (ethnic group), on the dependent variables COLIVA "Colored"-African values), COLIVA ("Colored"-Indian values), and INDAVA (Indian-African values), revealed a significant difference of opinion among the respondents on the similarity of values across race groups. The chi-square statistic ETHGROUP and COLIVA for instance, yielded a value of 21.369; with 8 d.f and a p value of .0062. Chi-square statistics for ETHGROUP and COLIVA, and INDAVA, respectively, yielded a value of 21.288 with 8 d.f; p value of .0064, and 21.937; 8 d.f. with a p value of .0050. (Also reflected in Table 5.6.)

Chi-square figures produced by a cross tabulation of the independent variable ETHGROUP (ethnic group), on the dependent variables COLIVA "Colored"-African values), COLIVA ("Colored"-lndian values), and INDAVA (Indian-African values), revealed a significant difference of opinion among the respondents on the similarity of values across race groups. The

Table 5.6. Responses on Similarity of Values Held by Various Race Groups

ETHGROUP	(n)	COLAVA	COLIVA	INDAVA
Mixed-Race	(11)			
Disagree		1(9.1)	4(36.4)	5(45.5)
Don't Know		4(36.4)	3(27.3)	3(27.3)
Agree		6(54.5)	4(36.4)	3(27.3)
Indian	(8)			
Disagree		1(12.5)	1(25)	2(25)
Don't Know		2(25)	1(25)	1 (12.5)
Agree		5(62.5)	6(75)	5(62.5)
***Sovenga**	(52)			
Disagree		33(63.5)	24(46.2)	35(67.3)
Don't Know		11(21.2)	20(38.5)	14(26.9)
Agree		8(15.4)	8(15.4)	3(5.8)
Xhosa	(21)			
Disagree		942.9)	6(28.6)	12(57.1)
Don't Know		7(33.3)	5(23.8)	4(4.9)
Agree		5(23.8)	10(47.6)	5(23.8)
Zulu	(35)			
Disagree		20(57.1)	16(45.7)	24(68.6.)
Don't Know		9(25.7)	14(40.0)	8(22.9)
Agree		6(17.1)	5(14.3)	3(8.6)
Total	(127)			
Disagree		64(50.4)	51(40.2)	78(61.4)
Don't Know		33(26)	43(33.9)	30(23.6)
Agree		30(23.6)	33(26.)	19(15)

ETHGROUP on COLAVA: Chi-square = 21.369; d.f. = 8; p = .0062
ETHGROUP on COLIVA: Chi-square = 21.288; d.f.= 8; p = .0064
ETHGROUP on INDAVA: Chi-square= 21.937; d.f.= 8; p =.0050
ETHGROUP: ethnic group
COLAVA: "Colored"-African values
COLIVA: "Colored"-lndian values
INDAVA: Indian-African values
*Sotho, Venda, and Shangaan

chi-square statistic ETHGROUP and COLIVA for instance, yielded a value of 21.369; with 8 d.f and a p value of .0062. Chi-square statistics for ETHGROUP and COLIVA, and INDAVA, respectively, yielded a value of 21.288 with 8 d.f; p value of .0064, and 21.937; 8 d.f. with a p value of .0050. (Also in Table 5.6.)

Overall, one can conclude that on the questionnaire items on values most individuals either disagreed that the values held by the various race groups were similar, or did not know enough about the values held by such groups to offer an opinion. This was a discomforting response as it indicated an existence of social distance between the various historically disadvantaged groups.

The researcher was curious to find out to what extent the various black groups identified with each other in the political sphere. As a result, items which prompted responses on the support (or lack thereof) the respondents would give to a political leader who is an out group member were included in the questionnaire. To examine such responses a cross tabulation analysis was conducted, first between the independent variable (ETHGROUP), and COLPRES, INDPRES, and AFRIPRES, acronyms for support of a "Colored" President, Indian President, and African President respectively. 33 respondents (26 percent) reported that they would not support a President of "Colored" descent. 26 (20.5 percent) did not know, and 68 (53.5 percent) responded that they would support a President of "Colored" descent. On the Indian President, 40 (31.5 percent) reported that they would not support a President of Indian descent, 23 (18.1 percent) did not know, and 64 (50.4 percent) responded that they would support a President of Indian descent. On the African President, 10 (7.9 percent) would not support a President of African descent, 15 (11.8 percent) did not know, and 102 (80.3 percent) responded that they would support such a President. (See Table 9). These results were indicative of the prevailing politics of the country at the time, which seemed to point to the direction that Africans were expected to play a role in the future of the country, and thus an African President imminent.

A discussion, however, of the meaning of the "don't know" category on the political support questionnaire items was imperative as in the preceding questions on values their number was large. On the questions whether an individual would support a president of a specific race group, a "don't know" response can be interpreted in a variety of ways. Firstly, a "don't know" could be an indirect disagree. Some individuals may found it safer to respond in a neutral manner rather than express dissent, particularly if the perception was that such dissent was unacceptable. Secondly, individuals could have been indifferent to the statement being made, meaning that it was not so important to them who became the president, more than the issues that such a person stood for, or represented. A collorary to this response could be that individuals did not know who they would support because they had not thought seriously about the issue and therefore could not predict what their response would be. The questionnaire item itself invoked several written responses such as the ones listed cited below:

... if one subscribes to non-racial principles these would be irrelevant (Respondent # 3).
If the person merits such selection (Respondent # 6).
I would support a leader who is committed to the struggle (Respondent # 10).
Not applicable. Irrelevant. These questions are meaningless (Respondent # 24).
The color, descent, or sex of a President is not as important as his/her political, social, and economic programs. I would support a President who understands and seeks to achieve the aspirations of all South Africans (Respondent # 31).
I will support a President who is elected through a one-person one vote regardless of color. (Respondent # 36)
... if it is the will of the people, a woman too (Respondent # 43).

In a country where race, legally, has been the major defining factor, responses as reflected above could be expected, and were both rational and logical. In other words, individuals rejected any statement or policy that influenced them, no matter how subtly to think and relate to one another as race categories. However, whilst the written comments indicated the intentions of the respondents, which ere to look beyond the race of potential presidential candidates, and focus more on the issues such individuals represented, a closer scrutiny of the group responses revealed a gap between the stated intention and real action.

Whilst the reactions by the Mixed-race and Indian group members showed consistency and consensus on the various response categories, some variation could be discerned among the African groups. For instance, 10 (47.6 percent) members of the Xhosa group responded that they would not support a President of Indian descent. (See Table 9). This response, by the Xhosa group, was probably due to lack of familiarity with the Indian group, since the majority of the Indians are located primarily in Natal, followed by the Transvaal. The Xhosa group primarily resides in the Cape Province. Furthermore, when one looked at the disagree category, there was a clear pattern of preference. Beginning with the Sovenga group, 7 (13.5 percent) of the respondents indicated that they would not support a President of African descent, 14 (26.9 percent) would not support a President of "Colored" descent, and 16 (30.8 percent) would not support a President of Indian descent.

Table 5.7. Responses on the Support of a President of a Different Race Group

ETHGROUP	(n)	COLPRES	INDPRES	AFRIPRES
Mixed-Race	(11)			
Disagree		2(9.1)	2(18.2)	1(9.1)
Don't Know		3(27.3)	3(27.3)	3(27.3)
Agree		6(54.5)	6(54.5)	7(63.6)
Indian	(8)			
Disagree				
Don't Know		1(12.5)	1(12.5)	
Agree		7(87.5)	7(87.5)	8(100)
***Sovenga**	(52)			
Disagree		14(26.9)	16(30.8)	7(13.5)
Don't Know		13(25)	11(21.2)	8(15.4)
Agree		25(48.1)	25(48.1)	37(71.2)
Xhosa	(21)			
Disagree		8(38.1)	10(47.6)	1(4.8)
Don't Know		2(9.5)	3(14.3)	2(9.5)
Agree		11(52.4)	8(38.1)	18(85.7)
Zulu	(35)			
Disagree		9(25.7)	12(34.3)	1(2.9)
Don't Know		7(20)	5(14.3)	2(5.7)
Agree		19(54.3)	18(51.4)	32(91.4)
Total	(127)			
Disagree		33(26)	40(31.5)	10(7.9)
Don't Know		26(20.5)	23(18.1)	15(11.8)
Agree		68(53.5)	64(50.4)	102(80.3)

ETHGROUP on COLPRES: Chi-square = 7.947; d.f. = 8; p = .438
ETHGROUP on INDPRES: Chi-square = 9.178; d.f. = 8; p =.327
ETHGROUP on AFRIPRES: Chi-square = 10.677; d.f. = 8; p = .220
ETHGROUP: ethnic group
COLPRES: support for a "Colored" President
INDPRES: support for an Indian President
AFRIPRES: support for an African President
*Sotho, Venda, and Shangaan

A pattern similar to the one presented above could also be detected with both the Xhosa and Zulu groups. Only 1 (4.8 percent) respondent of the Xhosa group would not support a President of African descent, 8 (38.1 percent) would not support a President of "Colored" descent, and 10 (47.6 percent) would not support a President of Indian descent. With the Zulu group, 1 (2.9 percent) respondent would not support a President of African descent, 9 (25.7 percent) would not support a President of "Colored" descent, and 12 (34.3 percent) would not support a President of Indian descent. (Also Table 9).

From the above pattern, one could deduce that a President of African descent was the preferred choice by the majority of the respondents, however, among the African groups, a President of "Colored" descent was the second choice, followed by a President of Indian descent. The response towards the President of Indian descent was ironical considering that all 8 (100 percent) of the respondents in the sample indicated that they would support a President of African descent. (See Table 9).

As mentioned earlier in this chapter, people's views and opinions are informed by their background and personal experiences, among which are their race or ethnic background, their age, and gender. Numerous studies have also indicated that the environment they grow up in, and in which they find themselves influences individuals' views, attitudes, and opinions. This factor revealed itself in the results produced by a cross tabulation between the independent variable, DURES (duration of stay abroad), and the dependent variables, COLPRES ("Colored" President), and INDPRES (Indian President). (Table 10).

The cross tabulation results reflected in Table 10 disclosed a difference of opinion between respondents who had been abroad less than a year, and those who had been abroad a year and longer in their support of a President of "Colored" and Indian descent. For example, 24 (45.3 percent) respondents who had been abroad less than a year, would not support a President of "Colored" descent, and 25 (47.2 percent) would not support a President of Indian descent. Shifting to respondents who had been abroad a year to five years, the majority—33 (61.1 percent) indicated that they would support Presidents of "Colored" and Indian descent. The responses of individuals who had been abroad six years and above read as follows: 17 (85 percent) would support a President of "Colored" descent, and 13 (65 percent) would support a President of Indian descent. (Table 10)

Also worth noting is that for individuals who had been abroad six years and and over, the "don't know" category was significantly smaller.

The chi-square statistical figures produced by a cross tabulation of DURES on COLPRES yielded a figure of 24.281, with 4 degree of freedom, and a p value of .0001.

The chi-square produced by DURES on INDPRES yielded statistical figures of 13.102, with 4 degrees of freedom, and a p value of .0108. These statistics seemed to indicate high significance.

Overall, while the responses produced by the cross tabulation of DURES on, COLPRES, and INDPRES were interesting, they were not surprising. They symbolized in concrete terms the impact of living under apartheid rule. For individuals who had just left the South African society divided along race lines, the inclination to be less open to leadership of a different race group member was stronger. For individuals who had been abroad longer, and who had an opportunity of interacting with a racially and culturally diverse group

Table 5.8. Crosstabulation of Duration of Stay Abroad Support of a President of a Different Race

DURES	n	COLPRES	INDPRES
< one year	(53)		
Disagree		24(45.3)	25(47.2)
Agree		11(20.8)	10(18.9)
Don't know		18(34)	18(34)
1–5 years	(54)		
Disagree		7(13)	10(18.5)
Don't know		14(25.9)	11(20.4)
Agree		33(61.1)	33(61.1)
>6 years	(20)		
Disagree		2(10)	5(25)
Don't know		1(5)	2(10)
Agree		17(85)	13(65)
Total	(127)		
Disagree		33(26)	40(31.5)
Don't Know		26(20.5)	23(18.1)
Agree		68(53.5)	64(50.4)

DURES on COLPRES: Chi-square = 24.281 ; d.f. =4; p= .0001
DURES on INDPRES= Chi-square = 13.102; d.f. =4; p = .0108
DURES: duration of stay abroad
COLPRES: "Colored" President
INDPRES: Indian President

of people, on a personal level, the inclination was to judge a person based upon leadership ability rather than as a member of a race category per se. In short, individuals who had spent more time outside of South Africa had a chance to interact with all sorts of people as humans rather than as race categories, and this in turn affected their perception of the South African situation particularly as far as race was concerned.

In exploring the research question on possible future conflict within the DSA specific questions were included in the questionnaire that asked directly about the extent to which the scarcity of resources, the presence of ethnic identifications, and class identifications could encourage conflict. To reiterate, human ecology resource mobilization theories suggest that as groups compete for access to similar, but scarce resources, racial, ethnic, class, and one might add, religious factors may be used for mobilizing membership, thus increasing each group's access to such resources. In South Africa, the fact that various groups were deliberately separated from one another, lent itself to potential clear and distinct, group mobilization along any of the boundaries already mentioned.

The most significant findings were on the questions on job scarcity (JOBSCAR) and ethnic affiliations (ETHAFF). A total of 73 (57.5 percent) respondents agreed that among blacks in industrial areas the most probable cause of conflict would be the scarcity of jobs. 21 (16.5 percent) of the respondents did not know, and 33 (26 percent) disagreed. On the questions on ethnic affiliations, 50 (39.4 percent) respondents agreed that amongst blacks in industrial areas the most probable cause of conflict was strong ethnic affiliations. 18 (14.2 percent) did not know, and 59 (46.5 percent) disagreed. (Refer to Table 11).

It is worth noting that the gap between those who agreed and those who disagreed with the statement on ethnic affiliations, was narrower than the gap between those who agreed and those who disagreed on job scarcity. The actual figures were 50 vs. 59 respondents on ethnic affiliations and 73 vs. 33 respondents on job scarcity conflict. In other words, among the respondents, there was more clarity on the role of the scarcity of jobs in stimulating conflict than there was on the role of ethnic affiliations. Clearly, competition for valuable but scarce resources stimulates conflict. However, the role and strength of ethnic identification in conflict was less clear. Sociological literature on ethnicity indicates that ethnic identification is situational and varies from time to time depending on what is at stake. Ethnicity is commonly used as a vehicle for promoting group interests by assisting groups in getting their share of scarce yet desired resources, such as jobs, education, and so on. Groups can pressure governments for allocations on a basis that is more effective than individual demands. Ethnicity has the advantage of combining an interest with an affective tie thus serving as an instrument that galvanizes groups to pursue their desired goals (Bell; 1975, Milne; 1989, Osaghae; 1990).

The socio-political dynamics being witnessed in South Africa at that point in the country's trajectory seemed to support the point being made here about group interests and ethnicity. The Inkatha Freedom Party found support in its predominantly traditional, and Zulu-based constituency, and the Conservative Party finds similar support in its predominantly traditional, and Afrikaner-based constituency. Both these groups, combined interest, or class, and ethnicity in negotiating/fighting for their demands. External agents also assist in heightening ethnic identification with the intent of achieving specific goals, such as categorizing people into ethnic enclaves and thus encouraging divisions among groups. The following comment offered in one of the questionnaires expressed this point quite succinctly:

> I think that conflict based on ethnic affiliations is encouraged by paper work [official documents] that consistently urges one to identify oneself by "tribe" or "ethnicity" (Respondent # 36).

Table 5.9. Responses on Probable Causes of Conflict

ETHGROUP	(n)	JOBSCAR	ETHAFF
Mixed-Race	(11)		
Disagree		2(18.2)	4(36.4)
Don't Know		3(27.3)	3(27.3)
Agree		6(54.5)	4(36.4)
Indian	(8)		
Disagree		4 (50)	4(50)
Don't Know		2(25)	2(25)
Agree		2(25)	2(25)
***Sovenga**	(52)		
Disagree		13(25)	24(46.2)
Don't Know		7(13.5)	5(9.6)
Agree		32(61.5)	23(44.2)
Xhosa	(21)		
Disagree		4(19)	11(52.4)
Don't Know		4(19)	5(23.8)
Agree		13(61.9)	5(23.8)
Zulu	(35)		
Disagree		10(28.6)	16(45.7)
Don't Know		5(14.3)	3(8.6)
Agree		20(57.1)	16(45.7)
Total	(127)		
Disagree		33(26)	59(46.5)
Don't Know		21(16.5)	18(14.2)
Agree		73(57.5)	50(39.4)

ETHGROUP on JOBCONFL: Chi-square = 5.835; d.f. = 8; p= .665
ETHGROUP on ETHAFF: Chi-square= 7.739; d.f. = 8; p = .459
ETHGROUP: ethnic group
JOBSCAR: job scarcity conflict
ETHAFF: ethnic affiliations
*Sotho, Venda, Shangaan.

In other words, when individuals are constantly asked to identify themselves in terms of their ethnic background, their ethnic consciousness is invariably encouraged, and strengthened, and could therefore be manipulated to achieve specific desired goals. Until recently, in South Africa almost all official documents required peoples' ethnic background as a matter of course, particularly from African people. Most documents required their ethnic background all the way to their forebears. As mentioned in chapter 1 there is no doubt that the ruling apartheid government had a stake in encouraging ethnic identifications, particularly among the African groups.

Referring to ethnicity as situational also means that there are times when ethnic identifications are not strong and even unimportant to individuals. If competition for scarce, yet desired resources stimulates ethnic identification and in turn group conflict, conversely lack of competition over such resources reduces the strength of ethnic identification, and in turn conflict. In point of fact, an appreciation of different ethnicities is possible where competition is removed and groups are in cooperation with one another. Similarly, individuals may be aware of their ethnic identities, and in a healthy manner, affirm them from time to time without causing conflict between themselves and individuals of different ethnicities.

Also, studies in ethnicity have tended to highlight its dysfunctional role. Ethnic identification can play a functional role particularly among migrants in that members from the same ethnic group facilitate the integration of new migrants to a new and unfamiliar environment. This process applies to either national, or urban to rural migrants, and international migrants.

Another finding worth highlighting is that a cross tabulation between duration of stay abroad (DURES) and conflict based on ethnic affiliations (ETHAFF) revealed significant differences of opinion on this issue. The chi- square statistic was 20.396 with 4 degrees of freedom, and a p value of .0004. Table 12, for example, reveals that 31 (58.5 percent) respondents amongst the 53 who had been abroad less than a year agreed that in industrial areas the most probable cause of conflict is strong ethnic identifications. A reverse response could be discerned among individuals who had been abroad a year and more. In the one to five years category, 33 (61.1 percent) of the respondents among the 54, disagreed that one of the probable causes of conflict is strong ethnic identification. In the six years and over category, 13 (65 percent) respondents among the also disagreed. From these responses there was some evidence as depicted in the responses of individuals who had just left South Africa that ethnic affiliations could play a role in stimulating conflict.

SUMMARY OF FINDINGS

In this chapter data collected from 127 completed questionnaires were presented and analyzed. The data were collected to address three questions raised about the possible nature of future conflict dynamics.

The first question addressed the issue of whether in a future South Africa conflict could be expected based on political and economic ideologies. The results of the analysis revealed that while the ANC received the largest support among political movements, this organization, however, did not enjoy the support an overwhelming majority. Only 53.2 percent of the respondents agreed that the ideology expressed by the ANC was the best for South Africa. The UDF followed the ANC in support given by the respondents. Responses on the BCM were more ambiguous revealing a split between those who agreed that its ideology was the best for South Africa, and those who disagreed. The PAC received less support from the total respondents, however receiving more support from the Xhosa group, and fewer support from the Zulu group.

Further scrutiny of the responses revealed that both the BCM and the PAC received the least support from members of the Mixed-race and Indian groups. A large majority of the respondents did not support the Conservative Party, the HNP, the Tricameral Coalition, the Nationalist Party, Inkatha Freedom Party, and the Labor Party.

Overall, the responses on political ideologies as reflected by black political organizations were diverse and widely varied, indicating an area of potential conflict in the future of South African politics.

A large majority of the respondents (88.1 percent) supported the notion of a future South Africa based on a one person, one vote, in a unitary state, thus indicating more consensus on this issue.

On the issue of the economic system, the majority of the sample respondents (66.1 percent) preferred a mixed economy for a future South Africa as opposed to a capitalist, socialist, or communist economy. However, a large

Table 5.10. Crosstabulation of Duration of Stay Abroad and Ethnic Affiliations

DURES	n	ETHAFF
< one year	(53)	
Disagree		13(24.5)
Agree		9(17)
Don't know		31(58.5)
1–5 years	(54)	
Disagree		33(61.1)
Don't know		5(9.3)
Agree		16(29.6)
>6 years	(20)	
Disagree		13(65)
Don't know		4(20)
Agree		3(15)
Total	(127)	
Disagree		59(46.5)
Don't Know		18(14.2)
Agree		50(39.4)

DURES on ETHAFF: Chi-square =20.396; d.f. = 4; p. = .0004
DURES: duration of stay abroad
ETHAFF: ethnic affiliations.

majority of individuals of Indian background (62.5 percent) preferred a socialist economy for a future South Africa. Again, overall there was consensus around a mixed economy system.

The second question addressed the issue of whether whites were likely to be targets of hostility from blacks because of past unfair practices. A large number of the respondents (70.1 percent) disagreed that blacks would seek to avenge themselves. Of the few who agreed that blacks would seek to avenge themselves, a large number of them, (88.9 percent) were male. However, 66.1 percent of the respondents agreed that if conditions for blacks did not improve at a satisfactory pace, whites would probably be targets of hostility. Of these, a large number, (74.2 percent) were of Zulu background.

The third question addressed whether conflict was likely to surface within and among the historically disadvantaged groups, and what the basis of such conflict might be. The results of the study revealed a presence of social and political distance between the various historically disadvantaged race groups which could pose problems in the future. On a social level, members of the various race groups generally did not seem to know much about each other's values. On a political level, whilst a president of African descent was the preferred choice for the majority of the respondents—80.3 percent, amongst the African groups, a president of "Colored" descent was their preferred second choice, followed by a president of Indian descent. Individuals, however, who had been away from South Africa a year and longer, revealed more willingness to support a political leader from a member of a different race group.

The majority of the respondents, specifically 57.5 percent, agreed that the probable cause of conflict in industrial areas was scarcity of jobs. Only 39.4 percent agreed on the role of ethnic affiliations. There was, however, a significant difference of opinion between individuals who had recently left South Africa, and those who had been abroad a year and longer, on the role ethnic affiliations played in the conflict found in industrial areas. A large majority, that is, 58.8 percent of the respondents who had been abroad less than a year agreed that ethnic affiliations played a role. On the other hand, a larger majority, which is, 61.1 percent, and 65 percent of the respondents who had been abroad a year to five years, and six and over respectively, disagreed. From these results one can conclude that whilst there was disagreement on the role of ethnic affiliations in conflict, ethnic identifications however could not be ruled out as irrelevant as reflected by the responses of individuals who had just left South Africa. Ethnicity thus could be expected to play some role in the future.

The analysis and results of the remaining two research questions is presented in Chapter 6.

NOTE

1. The ANC was founded in 1912 as the South African Native National Congress. Its name changed to the present African National Congress in 1925. The PAC broke off the ANC in 1959 over differences on the language of the ANC Freedom Charter. The PAC was formally launched under its current name on the 6th of April 1959. It was banned with the ANC on the 8th of April 1960.

Chapter Six

Data Presentation and Analysis
Part II

In this chapter the results on the remaining two research questions are presented and analyzed. To reiterate briefly, the said questions were: Is conflict expected between the homeland leaders, the citizenry, and the new democratically elected central government? In the event of a confrontation with the ruling government, can the disadvantaged group rely on the black middle-class for political alliance? The chapter begins with a presentation and discussion of the findings. This is followed by a qualitative analysis of the countries that have been suggested as the best models for South Africa. The chapter concludes by summarizing the overall findings of the 1994 study.

FINDINGS

Homeland Leader-New Government Conflict

The policy of homelands has been a controversial one since its inception in the early 1960s. As explained in the introductory chapter, homelands were conceived and implemented with the purpose of establishing a South Africa which was devoid of Africans, and which could then be declared primarily an area for white South Africans. Homelands were established under the pretext that they were the rightful areas of origin of all Africans, thus they could be turned into self-governing states in which Africans could exercise their rights. This plan, taken to its conclusion deprived Africans of their full rights in a country of their birth. Also, not only were homelands imposed on Africans by an unpopular South African government, their leaders were also nominated by the same government.

Needless to say, homelands and their governments have been viewed as illegitimate not only by the majority of the citizenry, but also by the international community. For this reason, items were included in the questionnaire that ferreted out the respondents' views on homelands and their leaders.

Not surprising, a vast majority of the respondents agreed with the statement that in a new political dispensation, homeland leaders should give up their leadership to new, and democratically elected leaders (DEMELEC). Of the 127 respondents, 110 (86.6 percent) of the respondents, for example, agreed with the statement. Only 14 (11 percent) of the respondents disagreed, and 3 (2.4 percent) did not know. (See Table 6.1). Interestingly,

Table 6.1. Responses on Homeland Leadership

ETHGROUP	(n)	DEMELEC	RESDELEC
Mixed-Race	(11)		
Disagree		2(18.2)	3(27.3)
Don't Know			1(9.1)
Agree		9(81.8)	7(63.6)
Indian	(8)		
Disagree		1(12.5)	
Don't Know			3(37.5)
Agree		7(87.5)	5(62.5)
***Sovenga**	(52)		
Disagree		6(11.5)	10(19.2)
Don't Know		2(3.8)	10(19.2)
Agree		44(84.6)	32(61.5)
Xhosa	(21)		
Disagree			7(33.3)
Don't Know			2(9.5)
Agree		21(100)	12(57.1)
Zulu	(35)		
Disagree		5(14.3)	7(20)
Don't Know		1(2.9)	9(25.7)
Agree		29(82.9)	19(54.3)
Total	(127)		
Disagree		14(11)	27(21.3)
Don't Know		3(2.4)	25(19.7)
Agree		110(86.6)	75(59.1)

ETHGROUP on RESDELEC: Chi-square = 7.382; d.f. = 8; p. = .496
ETHGROUP on DEMELEC: Chi-square= 5.203; d.f .= 8; p. =.735
ETHGROUP: ethnic group
DEMELEC: homeland leaders should yield to democratically elected leadership
RESDELEC: homeland leaders will resist democratically elected leadership
*Sotho, Venda, Shangaan.

75 (59.1 percent) agreed with the statement that homeland leaders would resist giving up their leadership to new and democratically elected leaders (RESDELEC). Another 25 (19.7 percent) did not know, a 27 (21.3 percent) agreed. (Also Table 6.1).

Stated differently, these responses on the two homeland questionnaire items indicated that while the concept of homelands was not popular with a vast majority of the respondents, homeland leaders were perceived as individuals who would not be willing to yield their leadership to new and democratically elected leaders. The two questionnaire items on homelands and their leadership did invoke written comments such as the following:

Homelands should be non-existent by then (Respondent # 1).
Homelands should not and will not exist (Respondent # 2).
Problem: Should homeland leaders exist at all?.. (Respondent # 3).

Only I hope homeland leaders will be given the opportunity to participate in "free elections." Presently they are having secret talks with De Klerk. (Respondent # 36).
There might be homeland leaders who are exceptions like "Holomisa" [Transkei] (Respondent # 50).

The dynamics in South Africa clearly indicated the discrepancy that existed between the hopes and aspirations of homeland citizens, and the political philosophies and directions taken by some homeland leaders. Homeland governments like Bophuthatswana, Venda, KwaNdebele, and the Ciskei faced spasms of uprisings from the citizenry who supported a new political system that included the formerly banned black political organizations. Also, some homeland governments, in particular, Bophuthatswana and the Ciskei, were known to have had a number of political prisoners who opposed both their governments and the South African apartheid regime.

Middle-class Alliances In The Event Of An Uprising

The South African middle-class, generally identified as individuals who have acquired higher education, and/or are materially well off compared to the general citizenry that lives in ignorance and poverty, has always been in a precarious position. Despite the existence of apartheid this group, has, however, managed to acquire some education, no matter how limited and inadequate, and material benefits. In the event of a confrontation with an unpopular government, whether the black middle-class could be relied on to give up some of its benefits, and join the most needy in challenging such a government, was an issue worth pursuing.

Existing literature in the social sciences indicates that the middle-class has played various roles in bringing down unpopular governments. As an example, in Cuba, Batista's unpopular regime was brought down by a group of individuals with middle-class backgrounds led by Fidel Castro. While the Cuban revolution had the support of the middle-class, after liberation from Batista's government, the interests of the middle-class were sacrificed in favor of meeting the needs of the most downtrodden Cuban citizenry. In most societies, intellectuals, specifically, have been the most vocal in challenging unpopular governments. The early founders of the African Nationalist Congress for instance were educated and came from the African elite. On the other hand there is indication that as individuals move up the socio-economic ladder, the less radical their political views are, and the more conservative their ideals become as they attempt to preserve some of the benefits given to them by those in positions of power, or acquired through hard effort.

In this study, questionnaire items on the black middle-class were seen as important, especially because the respondents by virtue of being abroad, and pursuing opportunities that most members of their reference group did not have, automatically made them a select group, whether they acquiesced to this label or not. The views of the respondents on the middle-class, to which they also belonged, were thus seen as crucial.

Cross tabulations of ETHGROUP (ethnic group) with COLORUL ("Colored" middle-class vs. the ruling class); INDIRUL (Indian middle-class vs. the ruling class); and AFRIRUL (African middle-class vs. the ruling class); revealed interesting results. On the cross tabulation of ETHGROUP and COLORUL the overall results were: 28 (22 percent) of the respondents disagreed with the statement that in the event of a conflict, or an uprising middle class "Coloreds" would align themselves with the ruling government whether black or white. 45 (35.4 percent) of the respondents did not know, and 54 (42.5 percent) respondents agreed. Similarly, a cross tabulation between ETHGROUP and INDIRUL indicated that 26 (20.5 percent) of the respondents disagreed that in the event of conflict, middle-class Indians would align themselves with the ruling government whether black or white. 41 (32.3 percent) respondents did not know, and 60 (47.2 percent) agreed.

On the statement that the African middle-class members would aligning themselves with the ruling class whether black or white, there was general consensus among all five ethnic groups. 72 (56.7 percent) respondents disagreed, 36 (28.3) did not know, and 19 (15 percent) agreed. The chi-square test indicated no significant differences ($p > .38$). However, an examination of the cross tabulation analysis by ETHGROUP revealed that there were significant differences between the responses given by the African respondents on the one hand, and the "Colored" and Indian respondents on the other. Africans agreed that the "Colored" middle-class members would align themselves with the ruling government (COLORUL). The "Colored" and Indian respondents on the other hand disagreed with same statement. (Chi-square= 31.5, p = .0001 on COLORUL). Similarly differences were revealed on the question of alignment of the Indian middle-class with the ruling government. (Chi-square= 21.5, p = .006). A summary of these statistics is presented on Table 6.2.

The category of "don't know" in these questionnaire items was also substantially high and thus required some discussion. To the author's mind, the respondents had difficulty responding to these questions for a variety of

Table 6.2. Responses on Alignments in Conflict Times

ETHGROUP	(n)	COLORUL	INDIRUL	AFRIRUL
Mixed-Race	(11)			
Disagree		7 (63.6)	4(36.4)	8(72.7)
Don't Know		3(27.3)	3(27.3)	3(27.3)
Agree		1(9.1)	4(36.4)	
Indian	(8)			
Disagree		6(75)	6(75)	7(87.5)
Don't Know			1(12.5)	
Agree		2(25)	1(12.5)	1(12.5)
***Sovenga**	(52)			
Disagree		6(11.5)	8(15.4)	25(48.1)
Don't Know		23(44.2)	20(38.5)	19(36.5)
Agree		23(44.2)	24(46.2)	8(15.4)
Xhosa	(21)			
Disagree		3(14.3)	4(19)	11(52.4)
Don't Know		6(28.6)	4(19)	6(28.6)
Agree		12(57.1)	13(61.9)	4(19)
Zulu	(35)			
Disagree		6(17.1)	4(11.4)	21(60)
Don't Know		13(37.1)	13(37.1)	8(22.9)
Agree		16(45.7)	18(51.4)	6(17.1)
Total	(127)			
Disagree		28(22)	26(20.5)	72(56.7)
Don't Know		45(35.4)	41(32.3)	36(28.3)
Agree		54(42.5)	60(47.2)	19(15)

ETHGROUP on INDIRUL: chi-square = 21.535; d.f. =8; p. = .0059
ETHGROUP on AFRIRUL: chi-square= 8.561; d.f.=8; p.=.3806
ETHGROUP: ethnic group
COLORUL: "Colored" middle-class vs. the ruling government
INDIRUL: Indian middle-class vs. the ruling government
AFRIRUL: African middle-class vs. the ruling government
*Sotho, Venda, Shangaan.

reasons. First, the questions were sensitive in that individuals were asked to express their views about other group members. People generally do not feel comfortable responding to sensitive questions. In the case of the respondents, who are also members of the DSA, this problem is compounded by the oppressive conditions under which they have been raised, whereby anything an individual says, can, at a later stage, be used to incriminate that individual. Second, the questions hypothesized a future event. Predicting how individuals will respond to a future event is difficult, one can only speculate. Rather than speculate, some respondents may have decided not to offer any opinion. The difficulty of responding to the questions on alignments, was best expressed in the following comment:

> . . . it depends on the nature of the conflict. For example, if the AWB rises up against an ANC government, they will get no support from anyone. If the black community rises up against a white minority government, they will get support from most groups (Respondent #3).

Third, a "don't know" may also be an indirect disagree. Again, on these questions, because of their sensitivity, some respondents may have found it safer to give a "don't know" response rather than a disagree, particularly if they felt that a negative response would not be proper.

The finding that a majority of the respondents, particularly African respondents, agreed that in the event of a conflict the "Colored" and the Indian middle-classes would align themselves with the victorious government whether black or white while interesting was not surprising. This perception was a reflection of the historical political and economic dispensation in the country whereby these two groups had received preferential treatment from the dominant group. Naturally, middle-class members of these groups are the ones who would have benefitted the most from this preferential treatment and would, thus, tend to want to align themselves with those in control of the country's resources.

A further scrutiny of the responses also disclosed differing views on the black-middle class by ethnic group. Members of the Mixed-race group for instance, were split in their responses to the statement that in the event of a conflict, or an uprising, middle-class Indians would align themselves with the ruling government whether black or white. 4 (36.4 percent) disagreed, and the same number agreed. 3 (27.3 percent) did not know.

Within the African groups, the general response was that the majority of the respondents either agreed, or did not know that in the event of a conflict, or an uprising, middle-class "Coloreds" and Indians would align themselves with the ruling government. This response was the opposite to the one given on the African middle-class, in which the majority of the respondents either disagreed, or did not know, that in the event of a conflict, or an uprising, middle-class Africans would align themselves with the ruling government. (See Table 6.2).

On the question of which groups would align themselves with the disadvantaged people in the event of a conflict, overall 56 (44.1 percent) of the respondent disagreed that middle-class "Coloreds" would align themselves with the disadvantaged people, 39 (30.7 percent) did not know, 32 (25.2 percent) agreed. Furthermore, 67 (52.8 percent) respondents disagreed that middle-class Indians would align themselves with the disadvantaged people, 31 (24.4 percent) did not know, and 29 (22.8 percent) agreed. Lastly, 23 (18.1 percent) of the respondents disagreed that middle-class Africans would align themselves with the disadvantaged people, 32 (25.5 percent) did not know, and 72 (56.7 percent) agreed. (Refer to Table 6.3).

Table 6.3. Responses on Alignments in Conflict Times

ETHGROUP	(n)	COLORDIS	INDIADIS	AFRIDIS
Mixed-Race	(11)			
Disagree		1(9.1)	5(45.5)	1(9.1)
Don't Know		2(18.2)	1(9.1)	2(18.2)
Agree		8(72.7)	5(45.5)	8(72.7)
Indian	(8)			
Disagree		1(12.5)	1(12.5)	
Don't Know		1(12.5		1(12.5)
Agree		6(75)	7(87.5)	7(87.5)
***Sovenga**	(52)			
Disagree		25(48.1)	28(53.8)	13(25)
Don't Know		18(34.6)	17(32.7)	15(28.8)
Agree		9(17.3)	7(13.5)	24(46.2)
Xhosa	(21)			
Disagree		13(61.9)	13(61.9)	3(14.3)
Don't Know		5(23.8)	4(19)	5(23.8)
Agree		3(14.3)	4(19)	13(61.9)
Zulu	(35)			
Disagree		16(45.7)	20(57.1)	6(17.1)
Don't Know		13(37.1)	9(25.7)	9(25.7)
Agree		6(17.1)	6(17.1)	20(57.1)
Total	(127)			
Disagree		56(44.1)	67(52.8)	23(18.1)
Don't Know		39(30.7)	31(24.4)	32(25.2)
Agree		32(25.2)	29(22.8)	72(56.7)

ETHGROUP on COLORDIS: chi-square = 29.983; d.f.= 8; p = .0002
ETHGROUP on INDIADIS: chi-square= 27.528; d.f .= 8; p = .0006
ETHGROUP on AFRIDIS: chi-square = 7.473; d.f. = 8; p = .4865
ETHGROUP: ethnic group
COLORDIS: "Colored" middle-class vs. the disadvantaged people
INDIADIS: Indian middle-class vs. the disadvantaged people
AFRIDIS: African middle-class vs. the disadvantaged people
*Sotho, Venda, Shangaan.

Again, a pattern could be discerned which was similar to the respondents' reactions on the questionnaire items on the black middle-class versus the ruling government. The majority of the respondents, especially Africans, disagreed that in the event of a conflict, or an uprising, middle-class "Coloreds" and Indians would align themselves with the disadvantaged people. Further scrutiny also disclosed differing views by ethnic group. Members of the Mixed-race group, for instance, were split in their responses on the Indian middle-class. 5 (45.5) disagreed that in the event of a conflict middle-class Indian would align themselves with the disadvantaged people. The same number agreed whilst 1 (9.1 percent) respondent did not know.

Among the African groups, a majority of the respondents either disagreed or did not know, that the "Colored" and Indian middle-classes would align themselves with the disadvantaged people in the event of a conflict. Again this response was the opposite of the one given on the African middle-class, in which the majority of the respondents either agreed, or did not know, if this class would align itself with the disadvantaged people. One factor which needs highlighting here is that for the Sotho, Venda, and Shangaan group, the number of respondents who disagreed that the African middle-class would align itself with the disadvantaged people was high. For instance, 13 (25 percent) respondents disagreed, as compared to the other ethnic groups.

Furthermore, among the African groups, a larger majority disagreed that middle-class Indians would align themselves with the disadvantaged people, followed by a large number of responses on the negative about the "Colored" middle-class. Respondents with a Xhosa background were evenly spread in their responses, that was, 13 (61.9 percent) disagreed that middle-class "Coloreds" and Indians would align themselves with the disadvantaged people.

A chi-square test of ETHGROUP (ethnic group) on COLORDIS ("Colored" middle-class vs. the disadvantaged people), ETHGROUP on INDIADIS (Indian middle-class vs. the disadvantaged people) respectively, also revealed significant differences between the responses given by the respondents. Figures for ETHGROUP on COLORDIS were: chi-square =29.983; d.f. =8; p= .0002. For the variables ETHGROUP on INDIADIS the figures read as follows: chi-square = 27.528; d .f. = 8; p=.0006. (Also Table 6.3).

The Model Country For South Africa

The last item on the questionnaire included an open-ended question that solicited the respondents' comments, reflections, and suggestions on a country that, in terms of its political economy, might serve as the best model for a democratic South Africa. Of the 127 respondents, 83 or about 67 percent responded to the question, and 44 left the question unanswered.

Among 25 respondents the running theme was that South Africa is a unique country that needs to carve and follow its own political and economic path. Some of the respondents felt that at best, South Africa could draw certain elements from the political and economic systems of other countries. The following is a sample of the comments:

South Africa is a unique country. Different models should be combined and then adjusted to the South African situation. No model can be taken as it is and applied successfully to South Africa (Respondent # 9).

No country at this point in time serves as a model. South Africa is generally unique (Respondent # 15).

I think that the South African situation is unique and that any form of government in terms of politics and economics will be derived from the needs of the country. U.S.A. for politics, i.e. one-person one vote and equality of all people. England for its social security system. Switzerland for equal representation of areas and people in government (Respondent # 21).

For now I don't know of any country that might be exemplary for South Africa 'cause every system is flawed in its way (Respondent # 34).

None. The South African situation is unique. South Africans have to sit down and formulate a just, democratic system that will address the effects of many years of a most racist system, as well as the multiethnic society situation one finds in South Africa. Aspects from the various systems in various countries can be used (Respondent # 75).

None. Both the socialist and capitalist countries are experiencing a political and economic downturn. One sinking boat is no better than the other (Respondent # 90).

None. Our political and economic system should be based on the concrete material and historical conditions of our country (Respondent # 92).

The best model would have been African. But since all of the African countries have been subjected to subjugation, oppression, and colonization, South Africans will have to develop their own model that will be best for them (Respondent # 96).

South Africa should create its own model and not be a copycat (Respondent # 97).

Must manage or mismanage our own affairs (Respondent # 103).

I would prefer an economic system in which the government (accepted by the people of South Africa) has substantial powers on economic affairs. This should be channeled towards a fairer income distribution . . . As the imbalances decrease, the economic powers of the government should accordingly be reduced . . . (Respondent # 110).

The idea of copying models to me is unappealing. As a country, the advantages (economic and political) given to whites should be given to all South Africans . . . (Respondent # 121).

Of the 83 who provided responses to the question, 58 (71 percent) cited a variety of countries that could serve as models for South Africa. Amongst these models, Scandinavian countries were most often cited as exemplary, with Sweden heading the list. Some of the reasons for the choice of Sweden included the following:

Sweden. The issue of language is addressed within the political system. Social services, for instance health care, is another issue addressed in the constitution. They have a type of democratic-socialism which seems to work well . . . (Respondent # 2).

. .. health care, welfare, and education are socialized, while the economy is primarily free (Respondent # 95).

. . . State intervenes in the economic activity, but does not fully take over the economy ... (Respondent # 42).

Second in line was the United States. The reasons for its choice were expressed in the following comments:

The minority rights (blacks) are protected by legislation, even if their chances of ruling are minute. . . (Respondent # 61).

At least America. It is slightly a free country in terms of political and economic freedom (Respondent # 63).

USA because to a certain extent its system is based on individual freedom. However, capitalist monopolies result in the dilution of those freedoms. (Respondent # 109).

Of the communist countries Cuba was cited with more frequency. Reasons for choosing Cuba were:

After the Cuban Revolution there has been an increase in health care for the people and an increase in education...(Respondent # 67).

. . . their ideology of socialism can be used to South Africa's advantage. . .This may help in overcoming the disadvantages incurred by capitalism (Respondent # 79).

Cuba. It is able to manage its own affairs irrespective of what other countries are saying or doing. There is less homelessness compared to other first world countries, e.g. USA (Respondent # 94).

Of the African democracies Zimbabwe was the primary choice. Comments on Zimbabwe ran as follows:

Their African socialism is working in the rural areas. For instance, the rural people of Zimbabwe are now producing more maize than before independence, and yet did not increase their ploughing fields, nor implement western machinery such as tractors. They have improved their traditional farming (Respondent # 23).

Zimbabwe has had similar problems as South Africa. Barring the effects of attempts to destabilize the country, Zimbabwe has done well. Most importantly, in Zimbabwe, whites no longer have fears of a black President (Respondent # 31).

Zimbabwe, for their reconciliation process. We can learn from their educational planning, also the process for returning soldiers, and their law too.. (Respondent # 107).

Other countries which were cited, though with less frequency, included China, the U.S.S.R., Singapore, Tanzania, the British Isles, United Arab Emirates, Switzerland, Britain, and Canada.

From the variety of responses given by the subjects on the possible model to be followed for a future South Africa, one can deduce that South Africa is so unique and complex that it was not feasible (nor even desirable by some respondent's comments) pointing at a single country in the world. During an informal conversation with the writer one individual expressed the thought that the question is challenging, in that South Africa is so unique, it is not like Europe, and yet it is not like Africa either.

SUMMARY OF FINDINGS

In this chapter data addressing the remaining research questions raised in chapter 3 were presented and analyzed. First, on the question whether conflict could be expected between homeland leaders and the citizenry, and the new democratically elected government, the findings indicated that homelands were unpopular with the majority of the respondents and that they had to be dissolved. Homeland leaders, however, were expected to resist giving up their leadership to new and democratically elected leaders.

Second, in the event of a confrontation with, or an uprising against the ruling government, members of the Mixed-race and Indian middle-class were perceived as members who would align themselves with the victorious group regardless of racial background. The same groups were also perceived as less likely to align themselves with the disadvantaged people, more so the Indian middle-class. There was, however, some indication that members of the African middle-class might also not align themselves with the disadvantaged people.

To sum up the overall results, the group of respondents foresaw a South Africa with an economy that strikes a balance between capitalism and socialism. Respondents of Indian descent in particular, indicated a preference for a socialist economy. There was overwhelming support by the respondents of the notion a one person, one vote, in a unitary state. Of all the political movements the African Nationalist Congress received the largest support—albeit not an over- whelming majority—among the respondents. They also foresaw a South Africa where, while blacks would not be out to avenge themselves for past unfair practices, whites would probably be targets of hostility if conditions for blacks did not improve at a satisfactory pace.

The findings also revealed an existence of social and political distance between the various black racial groups. However, respondents who had been away from South Africa longer than a year, showed a willingness to accept leadership from other race groups. The majority of the respondents saw the scarcity of jobs as the major source of conflict but there was indication, as revealed by the responses of individuals who had just left South Africa, that ethnic affiliations might also play some role in stimulating conflict. Implications of these findings are discussed in the next chapter.

Chapter Seven

Summary and Implications of the Findings

This chapter summarizes the 1994 study as well as its findings. It concludes with a discussion of the implications of the findings for a future South Africa as envisioned by the subjects of that study.

SUMMARY

Significance of the Study

To reiterate, history is replete with cases indicating the difficult period societies have gone through after gaining independence from external, and/or internal group domination. The change period from an old social order to a new one oftentimes is not a smooth one. For some societies the transition period to a new social order, and the period after independence, intentionally, or unintentionally stimulates old and otherwise submerged rivalries and divisions. Countries as varied as Zimbabwe, Mozambique, Nigeria, Haiti, the Philippines, India, Sri Lanka and so on have experienced problems of some sort after independence. After forty years of apartheid rule it would have been overly optimistic to expect South Africa to experience a smooth transition. Instead, the new South African society was expected to deal with old divisions that ran primarily on race, ethnic, and class lines.

The purpose of the study was to investigate potential conflict that could run along the above-mentioned boundaries. A review of the literature on conditions that stimulate transitional and post-independence conflict, an analysis the current dynamics in the South African scene, and conversations with South Africans raised the following questions that guided the study.

1. In a new South Africa was conflict expected based on political and economic ideologies?
2. Were whites likely to be targets of hostility from blacks?
3. Was conflict likely to surface within and among the historically disadvantaged groups?
4. Was conflict expected between the citizenry and homeland leaders? Between the homeland leaders and the democratically elected central government?
5. In the event of a confrontation with the ruling government, could the disadvantaged group rely on the black middle-class for political alliance?

Data used were collected from historically disadvantaged South Africans (DSAs). This sample of respondents was chosen for a variety of reasons. First, they were acquiring education, training, and experience that would be valuable in the creation of a new democracy in South Africa. Second, the respondents were a miniature representation of the views and behavioral patterns that could be expected of societal members who would play an important role in a new South Africa.

MAJOR FINDINGS

Within the limitations of the study sample, the following results were revealed.

Responses on political ideologies as reflected by black political organizations were diverse and widely varied, thus indicating an area of potential conflict in the future. The ANC, whilst enjoying the largest support among the respondents, however, did not receive the support of an overwhelming majority. Reponses on the BCM were ambiguous revealing a split between those who supported it and those who did not. Among the black political organizations the PAC received the least support from the total respondents, in particular from respondents of Mixed-race and Indian background. Within the Xhosa group a split was discerned between those who supported the PAC and those who did not. A large majority of the respondents did not support white political organizations. Included in this category were Inkatha Freedom Party and the Tricameral Coalition.

An overwhelming majority of the respondents supported the notion of a future South Africa based on a one person, one vote, in a unitary state. Consensus was also discerned on the type of economic system that would work best for a future South Africa. The majority of the sample respondents preferred a mixed economy. However, a larger majority of individuals of Indian background preferred a socialist economy.

The majority of the respondents disagreed that blacks would seek to avenge themselves for past unfair practices, however they agreed that if conditions for blacks did not improve at a satisfactory pace, whites would be targets of hostility.

One of the most revealing findings of the study was the existence and presence of social and political distance between the various black groups. On the social level, members of the various race groups did not seem to know much about each other's values, thus indicating a lack of real knowledge about each other. On a political level, whilst a president of African descent was the referred choice by the majority of the respondents, a larger majority of the respondents of African descent preferred a president of Mixed-race background as their second choice, followed by a president of Indian background. Respondents who had been abroad a year and longer were more willing to give support to a political leader of any racial/ethnic background based on qualification.

Whilst there was general agreement on the role of the scarcity of jobs in stimulating conflict, there were significant differences of opinion on the role of ethnic affiliations. A large majority of respondents who had been abroad less than a year, in other words those who had just left South Africa, agreed that ethnic affiliations played a role in stimulating conflict, on the other hand, a large majority of respondents who had been abroad more than a year disagreed.

Not surprising, homelands were unpopular with the majority of the respondents and there was indication as reflected in some of the written comments that they had to be dissolved. Homeland leaders on the other hand were expected to resist giving up their leadership to new and democratically elected leaders.

Regarding political alliances, the general response was that members of the Mixed-race and Indian middle-class would align themselves with the ruling government rather than the disadvantaged people. There was some indication, however, that members of the African middle-class would also not align themselves with the disadvantaged people.

Responses on the country that might serve as the model for South Africa were varied. Countries cited included Scandinavian countries, in particular Sweden, western and European countries like the U.S., Britain, and Canada. Also included were communist countries like Cuba, and African countries like Botswana and Tanzania. A substantial number of respondents however, indicated that South Africa is a unique country that needed to carve and follow its own path.

IMPLICATIONS FOR A FUTURE SOUTH AFRICA

From the study's findings it could be deduced that divergences in political ideologies would be one of the major sources of conflict in the future South

Africa. The existence of divergent political ideologies was not a negative per se because it reflected the various views held by a citizenry society that aspired for some sort of democracy. Intolerance of divergent political views however was the problem. South Africa's challenge for the future was in developing a process or plan whereby the different political organizations and parties could express their ideologies, and find new recruits without fear of reprisal.

Ethnic identifications were another potential problem area. Historically the ruling apartheid government deliberately manipulated real or imagined ethnic distinctions to achieve its desired goals. It appeared that even in the future this strategy could well serve certain individuals and groups. Ethnicity is part of a peoples' being and a healthy definition of who they are. However, under certain circumstances such self-definitions could become potent particularly when there is competition for scarce yet desired resources. In the future, candidates running for political office were expected to stimulate (intentionally or unintentionally) ethnic and even race identifications to gain membership. When the negotiation stage for a new South African constitution eventually began, some ground rules or code of conduct needed to be established, providing guidelines to all candidates for the type of behavior that would be acceptable during political campaigns. For example, intimidating language or "killing talk," racial and ethnic provocation needed to be discouraged.

Whilst there was general consensus on a future South Africa based on one person, one vote, in a unitary state, there was some indication, no matter how slight, of the wish by some groups for the recognition and preservation of their culture and language, in particular those groups who perceive themselves to be a minority. This was seen as one of South Africa's challenges in that culture and race, within the South African context, remain highly intertwined. A preservation of a group's culture and language could in reality translate into a preservation of a race group's privileges.

As some of the apartheid pillars got discarded, like the Group Areas Act, which prohibited individuals from residing in areas of their choice and financial means, the hope was that neighborhoods would become more heterogeneous thus reflecting the country's racial and ethnic mix. Equally possible was the recognition that some people would prefer remaining in their ethnic and socio-economic enclaves. In the social science literature, there is evidence indicating that upwardly mobile individuals given the choice prefer residences with individuals of their own ethnic and class background. This choice is described in what Milton Gordon (1970) referred to as ethclass group membership. A country like the USA, is a useful case study in which neighborhoods reflect the continuity of racial and ethnic groupings, thus revealing the persistence of discriminatory housing practices, or individual preferences in making neighborhood choices. A similar pattern could be expected to occur in South Africa. First while most groups opposed to apartheid welcomed the abolition of the Group Areas Act, which legally separated neighborhoods by race, its substitution with the clause that prospective residents should meet and adhere to neighborhood norms, was perceived as giving considerable power to local neighborhood authorities whose intentions were not always be noble.

The abolition of the Group Areas Act could have interesting possible outcomes in that well-to-do blacks could start to identify with the interests of individuals from their socio-economic background rather than their racial or ethnic background thus promoting some degree of integration. Yet, also, it was seen as possible that the same blacks could choose to remain within their own ethnic or racial neighborhoods thus slowing down the process of integration. This is an issue worth pursuing in the future with the aim of determining why certain individuals move out of their ethnic and racial neighborhoods, whilst others decide to remain in these same neighborhoods[1].

Whilst the abolition of apartheid legislation would be of use to middle-class blacks, a large number of blacks, in particular Africans, remained landless and poor. The abolition of statutory apartheid was only the beginning of the process of bringing about equality. Making the resources of the country accessible to all South African citizens regardless of race, ethnicity, and class was a challenge that would require a number of things. The first requirement was a sustained effort from all those in positions of leadership. The second requirement was an unequivocal commitment by all leaders involved in the change process, to the upliftment of all South Africans, not only special and favored groups. The third requirement was consultation with all relevant groups. Finally, constant and effective communication by the leaders with the general citizenry that implementation of some of the changes could take several years, was of paramount importance. Painful as the South African experience had been for all blacks, by charting her own path, as some respondents reflected, South Africa potentially could provide a role model for other countries to emulate in resolving race, ethnic, and class conflict.

NOTE

1. The point being made about mobility out of ethnic and racial neighborhoods by blacks, in particular Africans needed to be treated with caution. The emerging pattern indicated that well-off Africans were also moving out of their neighborhoods, commonly referred to as townships because of the prevailing violence and crime, and not for socio-economic reasons only.

Chapter Eight

Presentation and Analysis of 2016–2017 Survey Data

In the spring of 2016 the author took a sabbatical leave from her University and spent part of it in South Africa conducting interviews, and collecting data as a follow up to the 1994 study. This chapter discusses the responses received from the 2016–2017 survey and includes both quantitative and qualitative analysis of the data. The chapter concludes with a summary of some of the comments and input given by the respondents on countries that serve as best models for South Africa.

RESPONSE RATE

In this study approximately 100 survey questionnaires were sent electronically to prospective respondents. A total of 33 were completed, with 31 usable, yielding a response rate of a little over 30 percent. This percentage rate was expected because most of the respondents were being followed up approximately twenty years later. The majority were now immersed in careers that took them away from any prediction of a post-apartheid South Africa, with a significant number expressing despondency over where the country is at this point in its history. This despondency surfaced in some of the face-to-face conversation with the author while on sabbatical in South Africa. The running theme as reflected in these conversations was that South Africa remains work in progress, and at this point not quite the country they had envisioned particularly in addressing the now central economic imbalances in which race remains permeable.

Table 8.1. Demographic Characteristics of the Respondents (%)

Characteristics	Percent
Gender:	
Female	61
Male	39
Total	100
Age (years):	
< 40	0
40–50	19
> 50	81
Total	100
Ethnicity:	
African	84
Mixed Race/Colored	10
Indian	6
Total	100

Table 8.1 summarizes the demographic characteristics of the respondents. In general, a majority are female; compared to the first publication in which the majority were in their twenties, in this study the majority are in their forties and above, a large majority identifying as African, and residing in different parts of South Africa.

ANALYSIS OF DATA

Generally the survey questionnaire was designed to draw out the respondents' views on the current political economy of South Africa. The questionnaire items focused on the areas that remain pertinent to the South African landscape. These included views on the economic system best suited for South Africa, rural to urban migration, migration across borders, reactions of blacks towards whites, preferred leadership in government, and views on the black middle class.

A Likert-type scale was used to rate the responses in each section of the questionnaire with 1 indicating strongly disagree; 2—disagree; 3—don't know; 4—agree; and 5—strongly disagree (see Appendix E). The last item in the survey included an open-ended questionnaire soliciting elaboration and reflection from the respondents regarding a country that might still serve as a model for South African, two decades later.

KEY FINDINGS

Economic and Political Ideologies

To tap on the respondents' views on the economic system deemed effective for South Africa, including state leadership, a number of questions were asked in the survey. The following discussion addresses the reactions to those questions. The majority of the respondents (43%) disagreed that a capitalist system is the best for South Africa. (See Figure 8.1).This made sense considering that after two decades since apartheid was abolished, South Africa still reflects wide economic imbalances in which race remains pertinent. Research conducted by the author on the economic inequalities that currently prevail in South Africa corroborates this (Mangaliso & Mangaliso, 2013). It is intriguing that a majority of the respondents (50%) agreed that a mixed economy, part-capitalist and part-socialist system is the best for South Africa. (See Figure 8.2). Yet, a similar (50%) also disagreed that a socialist system is the best. (See Figure 8.3). For South Africa, capitalism requires tampering with some degree of government intervention in order to lift communities still facing economic struggles. At the same time there is keen awareness that government intervention will not solve all society's economic ills.

One of the emergent problems in contemporary South Africa is the increasing number of immigrants, particularly those from neighboring African countries. The outcome of their migration and participation in the South African economy has engendered xenophobia. The discussion around immigration follows a similar pattern found in most countries in the world that

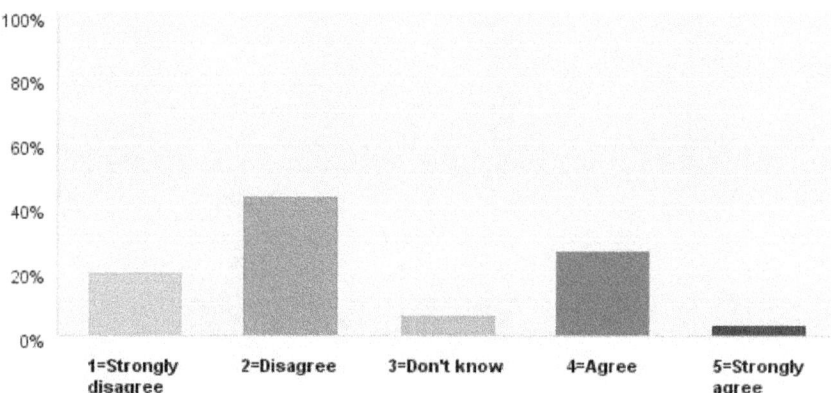

Figure 8.1. Preference for capitalist/free enterprise economic system

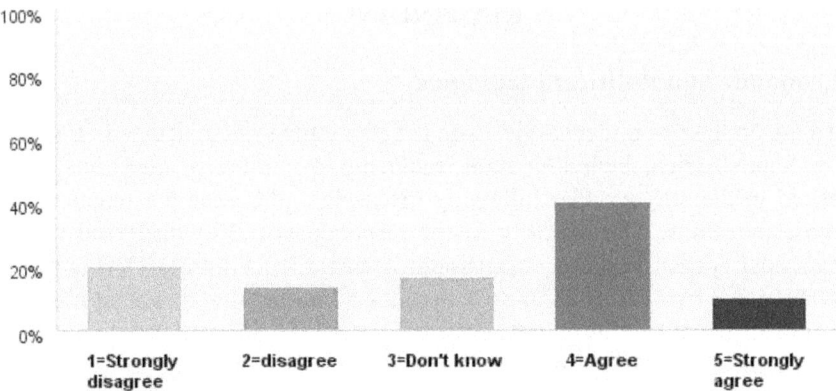

Figure 8.2. Preference for part-capitalist/part-socialist economic system

attract migrants who cross borders legally as well as illegally. Universally, the migration process is prompted by what demographers identify as "push and pull" factors (Yakey, 1982; Weeks 2012). Push factors are conditions that create stress, including lack of employment, educational opportunities, political suppression, and civil war, to name a few. Pull factors are conditions that promise to alleviate the stressors.

While a majority of African countries gained their independence from colonial powers in early to mid-20th Century, during the post-colonial era they have grappled with new political and economic challenges. Zimbabwe for example, a neighboring country to South Africa, post its own independence from Britain in the 1980s shifted from a promising bread basket case to a basket case (Moyo 2012)[1]. Consequently, a significant

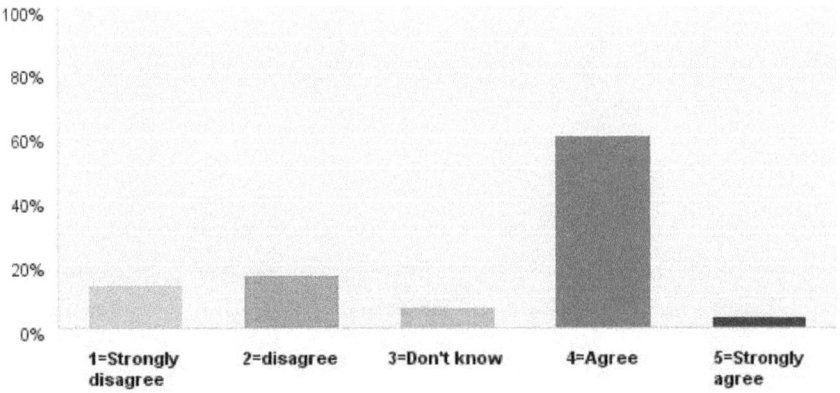

Figure 8.3. Preference for socialist economic system

number of Zimbabwean nationals seek economic opportunities in South Africa.[2] This has resulted in competition for job opportunities with South African locals expressed in the form of xenophobia. For this reason, the author included items in the survey questionnaire that addressed views and sentiments on the presence of foreign nationals in a newly emerging South African democracy.

The results of the survey revealed an intriguing pattern. The majority of the respondents (45%) disagreed with the statement that foreign nationals should be discouraged from migrating to South Africa. (Figure 8.4). Conversely, 57% agreed that unless skilled, foreign nationals should be discouraged from migrating to South Africa. (Figure 8.5). This tension surfaced in informal conversations with the author. There was keen awareness of skills shortages in key areas of the South African economy, which needed to be filled by anyone qualified regardless of national origin. Yet at the same time it was seen as only fair in the new South African democracy to speed up the process of developing its own nationals, particularly those from communities that had been deprived of opportunities because of artificial barriers created by the system of apartheid. This reaction was in alignment with the subjects' responses in which 53% agreed with the statement that in industrial areas, the most probable cause of conflict is the scarcity of jobs, while the same percentage disagreed with the statement that in industrial areas, the most probable cause of conflict is strong ethnic affiliations. (See Figure 8.6 and Figure 8.7 respectively).

On April 20th 1994, South Africans of all races participated in the country's first truly democratic electoral process. This process was all-inclusive in that all South Africans of majority age, internal and those living abroad had

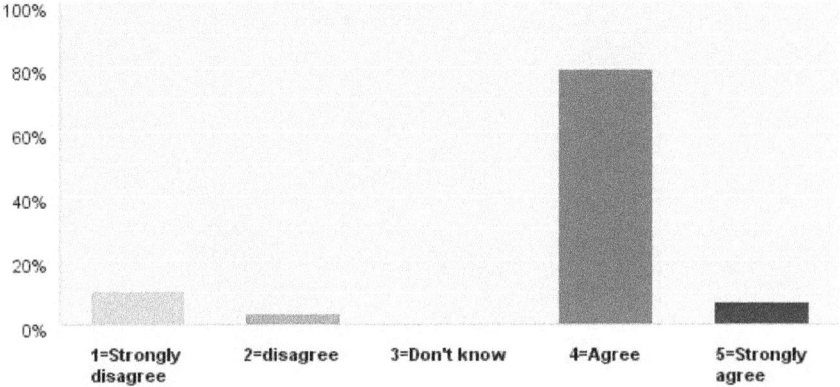

Figure 8.4. Unskilled foreign nationals discouraged from migrating to South Africa

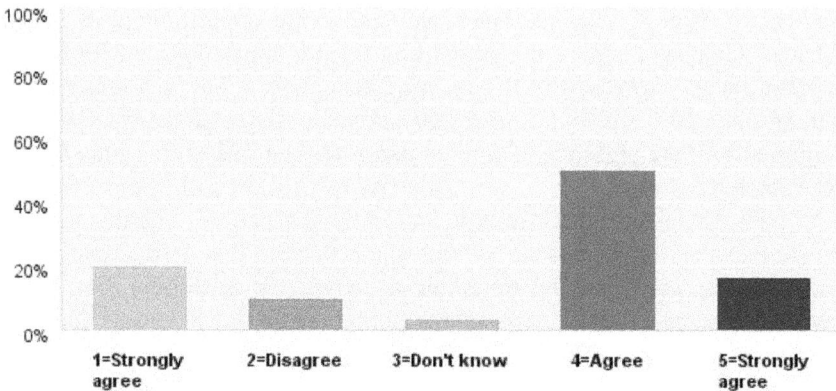

Figure 8.5. Unless skilled foreign nationals discouraged from migrating to South Africa

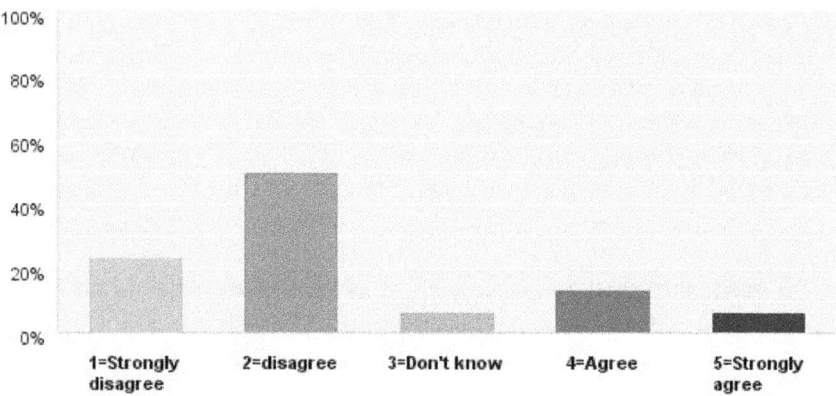

Figure 8.6. Scarcity of jobs probable cause of conflict

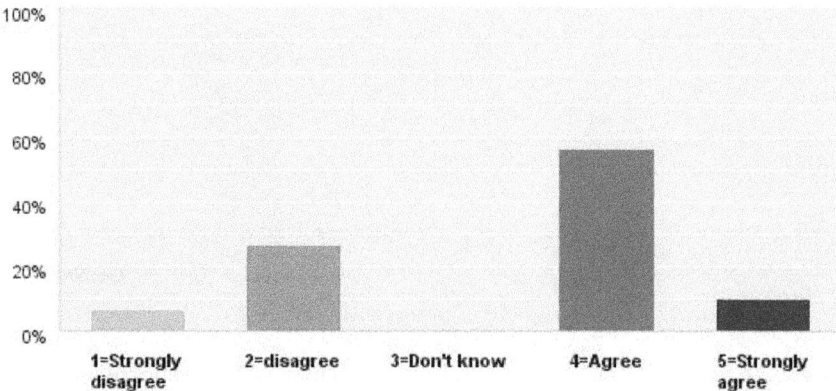

Figure 8.7. Strong ethnic affiliations probable cause of conflict

an opportunity to elect party representation. Nelson Mandela an African of Xhosa heritage emerged from the process as the first democratically elected President of South Africa. His party, the African Nationalist Congress (ANC) won the largest majority and later formed a government of national unity consisting of leaders from other parties as well. To the author's mind, the ANC's triumph during the election process made sense because of its inclusive language and ideology embodied in the 1959 Freedom Charter asserting that, "South Africa belongs to all who live in it, black and white." Since 1994 South Africa has had Presidents and Deputy Presidents who are not only black, but also African.

In this study the author wanted to gauge the extent to which South Africa is shifting towards political alliances not defined by race, particularly regarding who the incumbent occupying the highest office of the state, i.e., the Presidency, is. Thus an item in the survey questionnaire asked the subjects to respond to the statement whether they would support a President of "Colored" descent; Indian descent; or a President who is white. The majority (62%) agreed that they would support a President of "Colored" descent; 50% responded that they would support a President of Indian descent; and 40% agreed that they would support a President who is white. (See Figure 8.8, Figure 8.9, and Figure 8.10 respectively). While the sample size of the subjects in this study is smaller compared to the sample in the first study and publication, the responses are consistent. The subjects are informed, educated, and politically astute. In short, they factor effectiveness of the incumbent and how well they represent the interests of the majority of the South African citizenry. It is however, worth noting that responses of support for a President who is white, at 40% were comparatively lower. In the author's view, in a new South African democracy, it would have to be an extraordinary white incumbent to garner the support of the majority

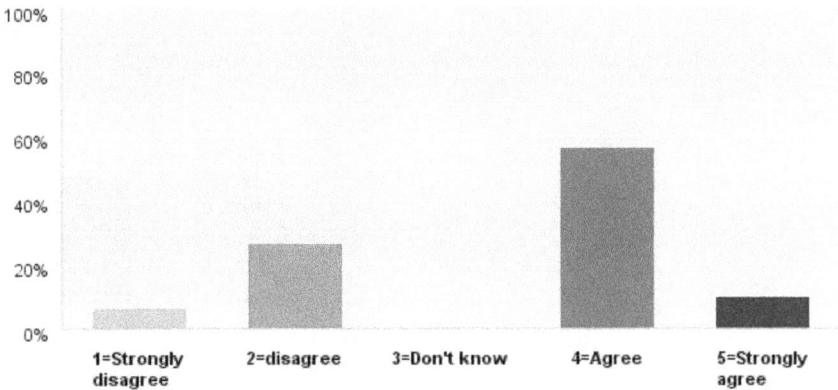

Figure 8.8. Support for a President of Mixed Race/Colored descent

Figure 8.9. Support for a President of Indian descent

of the electorate. The history of apartheid still hovers in the minds and conscience of the current generation.

Since the apartheid system privileged the white populace, the author was curious to know, with *de jure* apartheid no longer in the statutory books, whether in contemporary South Africa whites were likely to be targets of hostility from previously disadvantaged groups. On the questionnaire item that asked, "for the historically disadvantaged if conditions do not improve, whites as a group may be targets of hostility," 60 percent of the respondents agreed with this statement. A similar question focusing on historical political differences, elicited a higher response with 79 percent of the respondents agreeing that whites may be targets of some form of hostility because of historical political differences (Figure 8.11, and Figure 8.12). This reaction

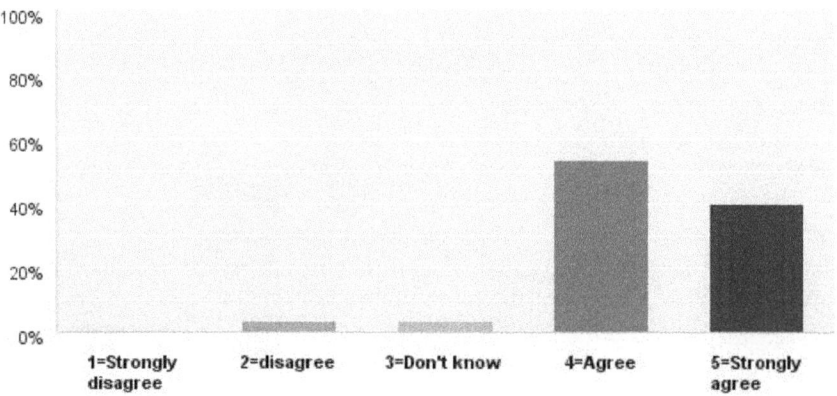

Figure 8.10. Support for a President who is White

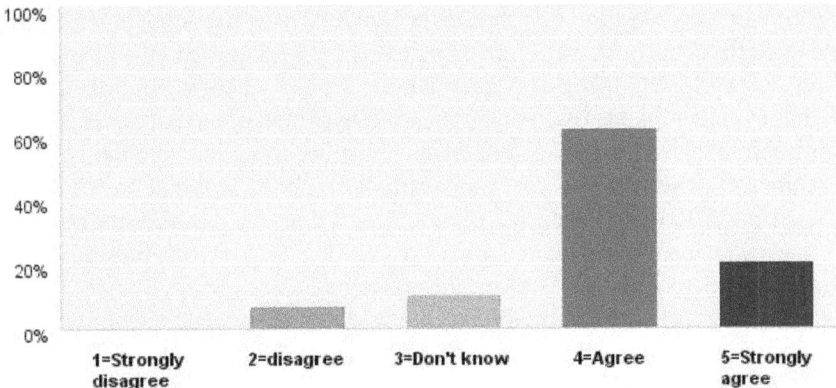

Figure 8.11. If conditions do not improve, whites as a group may be targets of hostility

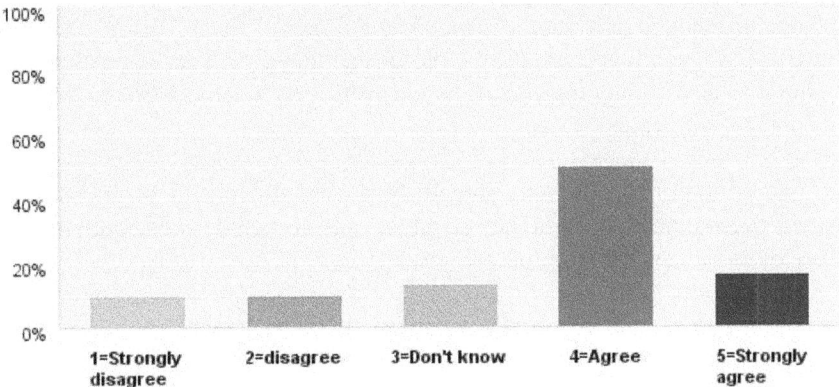

Figure 8.12. Whites may be targets of hostility because of historical political differences

overall supported the responses given in the study published in the earlier addition of this book.

The Model Country For South Africa

As in the earlier study published in 1994, the last item on the questionnaire included an open-ended question on reflections and suggestions of a country that in terms of the economic and political system, serves as the best model for South Africa to draw from as the country proceeds in the new democracy. The reactions were varied, with a majority indicating that South Africa still needs to chart its own path. The following are excerpts from some of the comments made by the respondents on this issue.

No country serves as the best model for South Africa (Respondent # 31).
No specific country does; South Africa is a very unique country. Nowhere in the world has there ever been an occurrence where a minority group that colonized lands of a people then implemented draconian laws that so disenfranchised its native inhabitants. I may be wrong but no other country comes to mind. Only to part ways partially with the political power it had over the natives but keep the economic and majority of lands/property in that country. We in South Africa are drafting a model on how to bring about justice and fairness as we go (Respondent # 5).
I don't know if there is a model. We have our own peculiar history and we need to create a model that will eliminate the huge inequalities and poverty. It should promote human dignity, ethical conduct and respect for human rights (Respondent # 3).
Not any one country. Maybe a mix of United Kingdom and some Scandinavian countries. Free enterprise together with government interventions to assist those who need help (Respondent # 24).
South Africa is unique and has to look for uniquely South African solutions. I don't know of any model that would work very well in a South African context (Respondent # 10).

A few countries in the African continent were also cited and the reasons why the respondents thought they could serve as best models for South Africa were discussed such as the following:

Botswana—it is a stable country, economy is doing well the value of their currency is even higher than the Rand in SA. In fact it is developing and growing (Respondent # 27).
History taught us that a single economic and political system is not ideal for the upliftment of society. Zambia is close to what South Africa needs. Unfortunately, South Africans were introduced to money in a very unhealthy way and they're now worshiping money hopelessly. Therefore, it will be extremely difficult to expect society to sacrifice today, and/or practice delayed gratification, while building a better future for all. "Social grants and free housing" system has created dependency and it is far from breaking the cycle of poverty. South Africa needs an economic system that allows government to create an infrastructure that provides basic employment for the majority, subsidize housing, education and health, and support entrepreneurs and SMMEs to flourish (Respondent # 18).

Countries in the developing world were also cited as possible models as reflected in the following comments:

Brazil. I think there are a lot of economic issues that are similar between the two countries. However I find that Brazil has a sharper and are focused attitude aimed at addressing economic challenges and holding the decision makers more accountable than SA and this will help shape it much faster (Respondent # 20).

China. The country may serve as the best model as it is a country that emerged from poverty and economic perils, to become a powerful and rich entity that continues to shape the economic, technological and political landscape of the world (Respondent # 25).

India. They share the same brutal colonial past, alienation from the land, and brutal removals as a nation. They were both subjugated by massive gun power. They both negotiated with the enemy to attain independence. They do not have short-term policies, but long-term view to develop their citizens. They did not follow the Nuremberg trial, but went through truth and reconciliation . . . (Respondent # 14).

Countries in the European continent were also cited, with Sweden being the most frequently cited as the best model for South Africa. The excerpts below support the statement being made here:

European countries whose governance serves the needs of society and support the government, health, infrastructure, and social needs of its citizens (Respondent # 28).

Germany—they have a socio economic balance (Respondent # 23).

Switzerland. Mixed economy (Respondent # 21).

Norway. Provision of social services to all its citizens. No poverty (Respondent # 1).

Sweden. For democratic socialism with narrow high-low income difference, good provision of the most important basic needs of the citizens (Respondent # 29).

Sweden. Any system that operates as a social democracy, where innovation and capitalism can thrive but not without checks and balances, and not at the expense of the poor. Requires huge investment in social support systems and capacity (Respondent # 17).

Sweden—women leave a better life and with good policies (Respondent # 15).

Sweden or Germany free education up to first degree; they have a thriving and stable economy. Sweden has zero crime and corruption. Both have developed rural communities (Respondent # 12).

Since all respondents had received college and graduate training in North America, it was not surprising that Canada and the USA were also cited as best models for South Africa. The reasons given for North America are reflected in the excerpts below:

Canada—has socialized medicine and democracy which is similar to the old South Africa, which did well economically but biggest problem was the apartheid system which is hopefully behind us now so we should be doing much better than we are doing currently (Respondent # 26).

Canada—It has a socio-political system that provides benefits to marginalized groups within this country. Given SA's legacy of discrimination and deeply rooted disparities, it is imperative to develop a social system that mitigates those historical disparities. In my assessment, a federal political system that accommodates the diversity within this country might the best alternative (Respondent # 9).

USA. Due to a free enterprise economic system! (Respondent # 20).

US political system where individuals are elected not the party (Respondent # 13).

United States because South Africa, like the US, is a constitutional democracy (Respondent # 11).

USA. Reasonably good access to participate economically and politically (Respondent # 7).

I guess the challenge is educating all of us about our new role in building a nation—remember we cut our teeth in activism through defiance campaigns and making the country ungovernable. How and when do we learn to engage in civic participation for good governance to build our young nation? What's my individual responsibility to South Africa's political environment and economy? Many still do not equate their personal decisions and actions to the economy crisis/impact the country experiences, we need to bridge that gap.

In terms of social support, I would prefer a modified version of the US system—mostly am interested in creating an incentive for work and financial contribution to the nation during one's most productive years as well as linking remittance support to other remedial/rehabilitation programs. More specifically, for the pension grant, there is no requirement or differentiation between earnings of someone who never worked or paid taxes a day in their lives and someone who worked all their life but barely making enough to save for a private pension—they all receive the same amount. The system needs to reward those who contributed and inspire currently employable folks to contribute to the system without eliminating the basic support to safeguard against poverty. With regards to the child grant recipients; since these are generally parents who are still at their productive ages, perhaps some vocational skills development opportunity so they may eventually be employable and graduate out of the social grant system. This need not be punitive but should perhaps be done alongside the provision of support, more of a well-rounded intervention perhaps with the help of civil society organizations supported or in partnership with government, otherwise we run the risk of creating lifelong dependency and miss the opportunity to restoring dignity by empowering people and communities (Respondent # 4).

NOTES

1. Moyo, D. Mediating crisis: Realigning media policy and deployment of propaganda in Zimbabwe, 2000–2008. Edited by S. Chiumbu & M. Musemwa. In *Crisis! What Crisis? The Multiple Dimensions of the Zimbabwean Crisis*, pp. 176–198. Pretoria, HSRC Press, (2012).

2. While Zimbabwe contributes the majority of immigrants to South Africa, a significant number of migrants originate from the West, East, and Central parts of the African continent.

Chapter Nine

Challenges and Possibilities of Bridging the Historical Socio-Economic Disparities[1]

with Mzamo P. Mangaliso

The running theme in previous chapters is the expectation of an improvement of the lives of the majority of the people post-apartheid. However, the surfacing reality is that while the new democratic government has delivered on the much anticipated one-person, one vote in a unitary state, economic prosperity and its attendant power, remain concentrated in the hands of a few. This emergent pattern appears to be similar to most countries in the African continent after gaining independence from colonial powers.

In this chapter, the authors grapple and reflect on the following questions; What went wrong? What can be learned from the South African experience?

SOCIO-ECONOMIC DISPARITIES

Reports by the Human Sciences Research Council (HSRC) indicate that the proportion of people living in poverty in South Africa did not appear to have changed significantly in the years following the attainment of democratic rule (HSRC 2004). Instead, households living in poverty seem to have sunk deeper into poverty, and the gap between rich and poor appears to have widened. That the disparity gap has grown faster than the economy indicates that poor households have not shared in the benefits of economic growth. In 1996 the total poverty gap was equivalent to about 6.7 percent of gross domestic product (GDP); by 2001 it had risen to 8.3 percent. At the same time, poorer households have not shared in the proceeds of economic growth—another manifestation of the rise in inequality between rich and poor. A popular measure of inequality, first introduced by Italian statistician and demographer Corrado Gini, is the Gini coefficient (Söderblom 2005). The Gini Coefficient ranges from zero where no income inequality exist and each member of society receives the same income (i.e., 0.0 = no inequality); to one where only one citizen receives all the income and the rest of society gets nothing (i.e., 1.0 = maximum inequality). With its inherited legacy of apartheid, South Africa has competed for the most skewed income distribution in the world along with other developing countries such as Brazil. But since the abolition of apartheid inequality, the Gini coefficient for South Africa rose from 0.68 in 1991 to 0.77 in 2001. By comparison, the Gini coefficient for Brazil dropped from 0.57 in 1995 to about 0.55 in 2002 (Arvigan 2006). Corresponding figures for the more developed nations such as Germany, Sweden, and Finland indicate relatively low Gini coefficients of around 0.25 in 2000.

A more intriguing observation is revealed in the Gini coefficients within each of the four major racial groups of South Africa, as shown in Table 9.1. Note that the white population had a Gini coefficient of 0.60, which is extremely high for a group whose education and occupational profile matches that of societies in highly industrialized countries. Note also that while in the past inequality was largely defined along race lines, in post-apartheid South Africa it is becoming defined increasingly by inequality within population groups as the gap between rich and poor within each group has increased substantially. For instance, between 1991 and 2001 the Gini coefficient for the African population rose from 0.62 to 0.72. Such a level of inequality is comparable with the world's most unequal societies. Increase in poverty in post-apartheid South Africa is further reflected by Osler's (2007) findings that by 2000, approximately one in 10 South Africans were living with less than $1 per day and one in three with less than $2 per day, figures that represent a statistically significant increase since the end of apartheid.

At first glance, therefore, it appears that democratic rule has truly taken hold in South Africa. In a short space of time, the government has taken on more responsibility in bringing about equity. For instance, unlike the constitutions of most countries, which confer only civil and political rights upon their citizens, the 1996 South African Constitution also ensured justifiable socio-economic rights for all of its citizens. Clauses in the Bill of Rights

Table 9.1. Gini Coefficient

	1991	1996	2001
African	0.62	0.66	0.72
White	0.46	0.50	0.60
Colored	0.52	0.56	0.64
Asian	0.49	0.52	0.60
Overall	0.68	0.69	0.77

Source: Human Sciences Research Council 2004

detail the obligations that ensure the citizen's rights to housing, health care, food, water, social security and education (Ajam & Aron 2007).

But upon further scrutiny these lofty goals were easier said than done, which the evidence from many regions of the country makes abundantly clear. The Gini coefficient figures above show that for many previously disadvantaged South Africans the picture has changed but little. Inequalities persist and, for some, the situation has become worse than before. This fact was confirmed by a study that reported that during the first ten years of post-apartheid South Africa real per capita household expenditures declined for those at the bottom end of the expenditure distribution resulting in an increase in poverty, especially extreme poverty, and inequality (Hoogeveen & Ozler 2005). This may be less than surprising since from ancient times democracy has always been partial and incomplete, favoring some and often bringing privileging to a smaller part of the population (Deetz 1992). Table 9.2 shows the extent of the discrepancies that persist in the quality of life among the different race groups in South Africa.

The disparities on Table 30 are supported by another study conducted by the South African Institute of Race Relations (SAIRR 2003). According to the study, the number of Africans who lived below the poverty line was approximately 62 percent, compared to 29 percent for Coloreds, 11 percent for Indians, and 4 percent for Whites. Disposable income levels displayed a similar pattern, with per capita incomes reported to be R7, 000; R13, 000; R36, 000; and R52, 000 respectively for Africans, Coloreds, Indians, and Whites. The percentage of distribution of the functional literacy was 65, 74, 88, and 99 respectively for the four racial groups. These figures are a stark indicator of the discrepancies that still remain, particularly between Africans and Whites. This fact notwithstanding, the African middle class, poised to take advantage of the removal of barriers created during apartheid, has been growing steadily.

Table 9.2. Inequality in South Africa: Selected Social Indicators

Social Indicator	African	'Colored'	Indian	White
Infant mortality (per 1000 births)	54.3	36.6	9.9	7.3
Female life expectancy (year)	67	65	70	76
Human development Index	0.50	0.66	0.84	0.90
Mean household income - (R '000)	17.9	22.6	40.9	59.8
Poverty rate (%)	60.7	38.2	5.4	1.0
Unemployment rate (%)	41	23	17	6
Access to piped water (%)	33	72	97	97
Access to public electricity (%)	51	84	99	99
Access to telephone at home (%)	14	38	74	85

Source: Moller (1999), DOJ&CD (1997).

112   Chapter Nine

As Table 9.3 shows, the number of blacks in the upper two quintiles grew from 15 percent in 1995 to 19 percent in 2011. However, in the process, a large black underclass continues to be left behind, with about 50 percent remaining mired in the lowest two income quintiles through most of the twenty years of post-apartheid government. The income gap between this black underclass and the affluent black middle class (albeit small) continues to widen, as does the gap in purchasing power between these groups (Adam, Slabbert & Moodley 2012; Mattes, 2002; Marger 2006). All of these are signs that much more serious reckoning needs to be done to avert problems that might accrue from a collapse of the middle class. If the conditions of relative depravation that currently exist remain unaddressed, they predispose people to justifying alternative courses of action, including violence or revolution (Gurr, 1970). We hope that in the case of South Africa, the trend will be reversed in time to avoid such an outcome.

Table 9.3. South African Income Distribution by Race in Quintiles, 1995–2011

Group	Lower Quintile	2nd Quintile	3rd Quintile	4th Quintile	Upper Quintile
B-1995	29	24	22	17	8
C-1995	16	22	34	25	13
I-1995	3	15	23	45	13
W-1995	3	5	10	60	15
B-2000	33	27	22	13	5
C-2000	15	23	25	22	13
I-2000	3	7	16	33	41
W-2000	3	8	22	60	19
B-2005	25	14	23	29	9
C-2005	9	14	24	28	28
I-2005	1	4	20	46	46
W-2005	9	15	22	19	19
B-2011	24	16	24	28	19
C-2011	3	13	26	43	21
I-2011	4	17	38	60	43
W-2011	2	4	17	60	43

EDUCATION LINK TO SOCIAL DISPARITIES

While education is generally regarded as a source of empowerment and emancipation, it can also be used as an instrument of oppression and disempowerment. For the better part of the twentieth century, successive apartheid regimes used education for the latter purpose. The apartheid-era educational disparities are well discussed in the literature (see Chisholm 2012; Fedderke, et al. 2000; Kallaway 2002; Kane-Berman, 1979; Litvak 1984; Mangaliso 1997). Some twenty years after the end of apartheid, and despite the government's progressive rhetoric, the promise of empowerment and emancipation has not materialized for the majority of South Africans, who continue to bear the burden of poor education.

A number of reasons have been suggested for this failure in education delivery, including high student-teacher ratios, poorly trained teachers, gaps between policy and practice, a lack of resources needed to implement the necessary changes, government bureaucracy underplaying or overlooking the realities on the ground in South African schools, and a bias toward political symbolism (Hartshorne 1999, Jansen 2002, Kahn 1996, Kallaway 2002, Manganyi 2001, Maodzwa-Taruvinga & Cross 2012). But it is paradoxical that a country with the wealthiest economy on the continent has a schooling system that is among the poorest performing systems in the world, ranking 140th out of 144 countries (Patel 2012). All of this highlights our thesis that while the goal of political rights and citizenship for all has been reached; profound economic inequalities continue to persist in post-apartheid South Africa. Since education is the spur for innovation, entrepreneurship, and economic development, it is incumbent on those in power to redouble their efforts in this area if the country is to become competitive in the global environment.

PUBLIC HEALTH ISSUES

One of the World's, and South Africa's, most vexing problems has been the HIV/AIDS pandemic that emerged in the 1980s. According to the UNAIDS global report 33.8 million to 46 million people worldwide were living with HIV/AIDS infections worldwide in 2005 (UNAIDS 2006). Approximately 25 million people living with the virus were on the African continent, with approximately 5.5 million of them in South Africa, where 20 percent of the adult population is reported to be HIV-positive (Mogotlane 2009). The impact on country's demographics has been devastating. According to the World Bank, life expectancy in South Africa has fallen from 62 years in

1990 to 48 in 1999 because of HIV/AIDS (World Bank 2002). The number of AIDS orphans—defined as children under the age of 15 years who have lost their mother or both parents to HIV/AIDS—has grown exponentially. According to UNAIDS, in 1999 there were 371,000 AIDS orphans and another 500,000 children who died of the disease. The Center for the Study of AIDS at the University of Pretoria projected number of AIDS orphans to reach 1.1 million in the mid-2000s and forecasts the number to grow to 2 million AIDS orphans by 2010 (Mogotlane 2009; Woolard 2002; Whiteside and Sunter 2000). Because of the premature deaths due to HIV, it is not unusual to find child-headed households with the misery that the situation brings to these children. The added strain on the country's already overburdened social services budget has resulted in the Health Care System's characterization as the AIDS Care System.

CORRUPTION

One of the challenges of newly independent developing nations is corruption. In most newly independent countries successive governments, hailed as the liberators after seizing control from their colonial rulers, have been brought down in part due to corruption. There was an optimistic expectation that South Africa would bate this trend. But this would hinge on the ability of the ANC to handle the transition from operating as a liberation movement to a ruling political party with the clear mandate of delivery of public goods and services previously denied to South Africa's majority. Even though the 1996 Constitution of the Republic of South Africa clearly states that the behavior of public servants is to be governed by democratic values and principles that include ethics, efficiency, effectiveness, transparency, and accountability, it soon became evident that these guidelines were not being followed as reports began to emerge that elected leaders were using their positions for personal gain. Nowhere was this more clearly illustrated as in the arms deal procurement scandal that broke in 1999 that involved people in the Presidency (see Crawford-Browne, 2004). There have also been cases of appointments or retention of underperforming and incompetent executives of public state entities based on their connection to the country's top leadership. A case in point was the ESKOM saga of the early 2000 where the underperforming CEO received support from the presidency in spite of the board's recommendation to have him removed (Khoza, 2012). Such behavior at high levels of government casts aspersions on how seriously the commitment to accountability and transparency is to be taken. Since upper-level leaders in any organization role model the behavior of lower level managers, it comes as no surprise that elected officers at all levels of government around the country were also involved in corruption of one form or another (Atkinson 2012). In the criminal justice system corrupt officers are said to have granted thousands of convicted criminals licenses to own firearms, and others were allowing prisoners to escape at the rate of about 100 each month (Adam, Slabbert & Moodley 2012). Upon their return, these freed criminals wreak havoc on civil society with a heavier impact on the most vulnerable citizens as discussed in the next section. Corruption in South Africa as a whole has been steadily on the rise in the period following democratic rule (see Transparency International, 2012[2]). Part of the problem may be due to a loss of what Khoza (2012) calls *attuned leadership*, that is leadership that is committed to the common good of society as a whole rather than to the self. It is the kind of leadership that exhibits humility, connectedness, compassion, and reasonableness. All of these are characteristics embodied in the philosophy of Ubuntu, which has found its way into the worldwide scholarly discourse largely led by Southern African writers and thinkers (see Khoza, 1996, 2012; Makgoba 2001, Mangaliso, 2001; Mbigi & Maree, 1995; Mnyaka & Mothlabi, 2007; Prinsloo, 1994; Ramose, 1999; Setiloane, 1986; Shutte, 2001). It is lamentable, therefore, that even though the leadership is quite aware of the positive influences of Ubuntu but seems to use them as instruments for power rather than situating them at the base or foundation of their behaviors and actions.

CRIME AND VIOLENCE

Post-apartheid South Africa also suffers from mounting crime and violence. The most vulnerable targets have been women and children with rape—one of the most grievous human rights violations and serious public health issues—occurring with regularity in South Africa. Police records indicate that 54,000 rapes or 150 per day were reported in 2006. According to the Medical Research Council of South Africa, most of the victims were young women between 16 and 25 years (Christofides, et al. 2006). But this seriously understates the problem as many incidents go unreported. One of apartheid's most deleterious effects of apartheid is that men felt emasculated and humiliated. They would take out their frustrations on the weakest victims—women and children. That trend seems to have continued into post-apartheid South Africa, where one unfortunate public health consequence of rape is an opportunity for the direct transmission of HIV.

NEW GOVERNMENT
PROGRAMS TO RESTORE EQUITY

The social and economic inequalities that had characterized the apartheid era have continued to dog South Africa in the post-apartheid era as well. At the onset of democratic rule in 1994 the country adopted an interim constitution, made permanent in 1996 that emphasized fiscal prudence, accountability and transparency within all three branches of government. The Public Finance Management Act (PFMA) of 1999 to gave voice to the constitutional imperatives of budgetary efficiency and fiscal transparency. A key characteristic of the PFMA was the institution of the Medium Term Expenditure Framework (MTEF) with its provision for three-year rolling budgets to guide and monitor the responses to priorities with greater timeliness and responsiveness. With the passage of the PFMA, the emphasis shifted from an input-output oriented system towards a more outcome- and impact- oriented system (Ajam and Aron 2007). Soon after the election, the new ANC-led Government of National Unity (GNU) introduced its first program of reform, the Reconstruction and Development Program (RDP). Released in 1994, the document pledged to meet the country's basic needs in a consultative, people-driven manner with an emphasis on Keynesian-type redistribution and economic growth. It represented tangible evidence that the GNU was serious about redressing past injustices and inequalities and eradicating the poverty afflicting a significant number of the 40 million blacks who constituted the majority of South Africa's population (Hart 2002). To ensure its effectiveness, an RDP Office established within the Office of the President held responsibility for coordinating RDP-related activities across the country.

But in early 1996, amid much public debate over what the program meant for economic policy, the RDP Office was closed down and its staff redeployed to other government departments. At about the same time, the government introduced a new, neo-liberal initiative called the Growth, Employment, and Redistribution (GEAR) program. The business community applauded the program because of its emphasis on fiscal restraint, its expressed commitment to controlling inflation and interest rates, and the promise of relaxed foreign exchange controls. Philosophically, GEAR uncomfortably sat astride the emancipatory promises of the liberation struggle on the one hand, and the material hopes, aspirations, and rights of the black majority on the other (Hart 2002). And according to some analysts, because of its neo-market-oriented policy, GEAR seemed to serve the interests of those who already had the wherewithal to take advantage of the lucrative opportunities in place for procuring government contracts (Avirgan 2006). GEAR is thus seen to benefit only a few blacks, while offering little or nothing to a large majority.

Another government initiative that addressed the wealth distribution problem was the Black Economic Empowerment (BEE) program. BEE was a flagship program intended to accelerate the participation rate of blacks in the country's economy without disturbing the fundamentals of the market enterprise system. As a form of affirmative action, BEE was seen as the best hope for compensating for apartheid's negative legacy, thereby accomplishing ownership and employment equity in the workplace (McFarlin et al. 1999). True enough, some progress has ensued in the form of a steady rise in both the number and size of corporations owned or controlled by blacks since the mid-1990s. For instance, through mergers and acquisitions, Metlife became the largest black empowerment investment in the financial services sector as of 1999, making it the 26th largest company on the Johannesburg Stock Exchange (Southall 2004). Various sectors of the economy—media, forestry and paper pulp, food and beverages, or fishing—have all attracted large-scale black investments (Carter, 2000). In spite of these indications of success, progress made has been modest, uneven and difficult to quantify. Of concern, a significant number of South Africans have remained skeptical of BEE, viewing it as problematic with some going as far as calling it discrimination, or reverse racism. To complicate matters, BEE, in its implementation became mired in problems that resulted in the slow growth of genuinely entrepreneurial blacks. Accompanying problems included a lack of start-up capital, the closed nature of business fraternities, fronting, and corruption. Unfortunately the program has drawn into the economic mainstream only a handful of politically connected blacks who, in a short space of time, have become remarkably wealthy (Southall 2004). Below Randall (1996: 662) cites some of the more prominent voices that have been critical of the emerging class of black capitalists in South Africa.

> The rise (of the black capitalist class) is perceived to be part of 'a cosmetic attempt to dress up old apartheid structures of power and priviledge,' so as to 'maintain the status quo, lipsticked and pretified. The result, the argument goes, is that black capitalists are not genuine capitalists, having 'nothing more than a press-release understanding of the company,' surrounding themselves 'with white advisors and consultants who then run the company by remote control while they are left to indulge in the life of the *nouveau riche*.' Senior black managers are 'hired for their compliance and for their smiling faces in our corporate brochures,' or to act as 'the gopher: get the business in, smile, shake hands, and then leave it to us to get on with the job.' Whites, it is asserted, have assured at all costs that their black lackeys 'don't ever get involved in our core business issues.'

From these observations, the BEE program appeared to be headed towards GEAR's unhappy fate. To mitigate this, the program was revised and expanded to draw in community groups and employee trusts as participants in the preferential contract procurement framework. The revised program was codified into law as the Broad Based Black Economic Empowerment Act (BBBEE) of 2003. The jury is still out over whether the new BBBEE program will yield the desired outcomes.

SUMMARY AND CONCLUSION

It has been just over two decades since apartheid was put in the dustbin of history in South Africa. That itself has been an achievement marked by the release of Nelson Mandela from 27 years of imprisonment from Robben Island, the unbanning of all formerly banned political movements, the release of all other political prisoners, and an opportunity to return to South Africa by individuals exiled because of apartheid. Consequently, a generation of a category of citizens are emerging who did not directly experience the ravages of apartheid, and appropriately dubbed as "born frees." In short, South Africa is no longer ruled by a white minority government steeped in racist ideology. All South Africans of majority age ushered a historical day (April 27, 1994), when they voted for the first democratic government led by Nelson Mandela, and the ANC. The anniversary day of this historical moment is now a public holiday—Freedom Day.

Based on the findings and discussions in this book, it is clear that South Africa remains a beacon of hope. All citizens have access to political power and enjoy political efficacy in that if they chose to, they can participate in the political process at all levels, in immediate communities, at municipal, province, and state level. What South Africa continues to grapple with is spreading its economic pie so the majority of the people down the generations see improvement in their lives.

NOTES

1. Earlier versions of this chapter, co-authored with Mzamo P. Mangaliso, were presented and published at the 2012 American Sociological Association Meetings in Las Vegas, NE; 2011 International Eastern Academy of Management in Bangalore, India; and the *Journal of Black Studies, 44, 5 (2015), 529-546*. The financial support of our institutions is acknowledged.

2. Transparency International (TI) is a group that monitors, on an annual basis, the corruption levels of different countries worldwide. TI's Corruption Perception Index (CPI) measures the corruption level in the country's public services as perceived by a panel of worldwide analysts, experts and executives. The less corrupt the country, the higher the ranking. TI reports show that South Africa has followed a downward spiral in terms of the CPI, from being ranked 21st in 1995, to 38th in 2001, 46th in 2005, 54th in 2010, and 69th in 2012.

Appendix A
Acronyms of Variables in the Questionnaire

QUESTION	VARIABLE	ACRONYM
16	Capitalist economic system	CAPEC
17	Part-capitalist/Part-socialist economic system	CAPSOC
18	Socialist economic system	SOCEC
19	Communist economic system	COMEC
20	Rural people and job guarantees	RURJOB
21	Rural-urban behavior	RURBEH
22	Rural standards	RURSTAN
23	Urban superiority	URBSUP
24	Ethnic affiliations	ETHAFF
25	Job scarcity conflict	JOBCONFL
26	One person one vote	ONEVOT
27	Group rights	GROUPRI
28	Partitioning of states	PARTIT
29	Blacks avenging themselves	AVENGE
30	Black vs. white group hostility	GROUPAT
31	Individual white attack	INDIVAT
32	Black vs. white historical differences	HISTODIF
33	"Colored" President	COLPRES
34	Indian President	INDPRES
35	African President	AFRIPRES
36	"Colored"-African values	COLAVA
37	"Colored"-Indian values	COLIVA
38	Indian-African values	INDAVA
39	Right to live in exclusive areas	RILTVEX
40	African Nationalist Congress	ANC
41	Black Consciousness Movement	BCM

(continued)

QUESTION	VARIABLE	ACRONYM
42	Conservative Party	CP
43	Democratic Party	DP
44	Herstige Nasionale Party	HNP
45	Inkatha Freedom Party	IFP
46	Labor Party	LP
47	Natal Indian Congress	NIC
48	Nationalist Party	NP
49	Pan-Africanist Party	PAC
50	Tricameral Coalition	TC
51	United Democratic Party	UDF
52	Democratically elected leadership	DEMELEC
53	Resist democratically elected leadership	RESDELEC
54	Educated-uneducated differences	EDUCDIF
55	Well-off vs. less well off	ECONDTFF
56	Race power struggle	RACESTR
57	Educated vs. uneducated power struggle	EDUCSTR
58	"Colored"-Indian lifestyle	COLINLIF
59	"Colored"-Indian politics	COLINPOL
60	"Colored"-African lifestyle	COAFLIFE
61	"Colored" - African politics	COAFPOL
62	Indian- African lifestyle	TNAFLIFE
63	Indian-African politics	INAFPOL
64	Middle vs. lower-class differences	MICLODIF
65	"Colored" middle-class vs. the ruling government	COLORUL
66	Indian middle-class vs. the ruling government	INDIRUL
67	African middle-class vs. the ruling government	AFRIRUL
68	"Colored" middle-class vs. the disadvantaged people	COLORDIS
69	Indian middle-class vs. the disadvantaged people	INDIADIS
70	African middle-class vs. the disadvantaged people	AFRIDIS

Appendix B

List of Abbreviations: Some Historical Political Parties

Party	Abbreviation
African Nationalist Congress	ANC
Black Consciousness Movement	BCM
Conservative Party	CP
Democratic Party	DP
Herstigte Nasionale Party	HNP
Inkatha Freedom Party	IFP
Labor Party	LP
Natal Indian Congress	NIC
Nationalist Party	NP
Pan-Africanist Congress	PAC
Tricameral Coalition	TC
United Democratic Front	UDF

Appendix C

List of Political Parties Represented In Parliament in a Democratic South Africa 2016

Party	Abbreviation
African Christian Democratic Party	ACDP
African Independent Congress	AIC
African National Congress	ANC
African Peoples' Convention	APC
Agang South Africa	Agang
Congress of the People	COPE
Democratic Alliance	DA
Economic Freedom Fighters	EFF
Freedom Front Plus	FF
Inkatha Freedom Party	IFP
National Freedom Party	NFP
Pan Africanist Congress	PAC
United Democratic Movement	UDM

Appendix D
Questionnaire

Demographic Information
In this section a few questions are asked about yourself. Please answer them as precisely as you can.

1. Which province do you come from in South Africa?
   a. Cape Province
   b. Natal
   c. Orange Free State
   d. Transvaal.

2. Which city or town? _____

3. Which suburb or township? _____

4. Which languages do you speak? Please rank in order of fluency, from most fluent to least fluent.
   a. _____
   b. _____
   c. _____
   d. _____
   e. _____

5. Where do your parents originate from in South Africa?
   a. Name of city or town_____
   b. Name of province_____
   c. Name of countryside/rural area_____

6. Which languages do your parents speak fluently?_____

7. What is the ethnic background of each of your parents? (Example: Xhosa, Zulu, Sotho, French, etc.)
   Mother _____
   Father _____

8. How long have you been in the U.S./ Britain/Canada?
   a. 0–5 months
   b. 6–11 months
   c. 1–5 years
   d. 6–10 years
   e. Over 10 years

9. Field of study /expertise
   a. Engineering/Computers
   b. Social sciences
   c. Business
   d. Natural Sciences
   e. Education
   f. Health
   g. Other (Specify) _____

10. Age
    a. Less than 21
    b. 21–30
    c. 31–40
    d. 41–50
    e. 51 and above

11. Gender
    a. Female
    b. Male

12. Marital status
    a. Married
    b. Engaged
    c. Single
    d. Divorced
    e. Widowed

13. Please indicate the ethnic background of your partner. (Example: Xhosa, Zulu, Sotho, French, etc.)

14. How are you classified by the South African government?_____
    a. "Colored"
    b. African
    c. Asian
    d. Nguni
    e. Sotho
    f. Black
    g. Other (Specify)_____

15. How do you identify yourself?
    a. "Colored"
    b. African
    c. Asian
    d. Nguni
    e. Sotho
    f. Black
    g. Other (Specify)_____

To the following questions please indicate your response in the following manner:

1 = Strongly disagree; 2 = Disagree; 3 = Don't know; 4 = Agree; 5 = Strongly agree.

16. A capitalist/free enterprise economic system will work best for South Africa.   1 2 3 4 5

17. A part-capitalist/part-socialist economic system will work best for South Africa.   1 2 3 4 5

18. A socialist economic system will work best for South Africa.   1 2 3 4 5

19. A communist economic system will work best for South Africa.   1 2 3 4 5

20. Rural people should be discouraged from migrating to urban areas unless jobs can be guaranteed for them.   1 2 3 4 5

21. In urban areas, rural migrants behave better than urban people.   1 2 3 4 5

22. Rural people lower the general standards of living in urban areas.   1 2 3 4 5

23. Urban people have a tendency to view themselves as superior to rural people.   1 2 3 4 5

24. Among blacks in industrial areas the most probable cause of conflict is strong ethnic affiliations. 1 2 3 4 5
25. Among blacks in industrial areas the most probable cause of conflict is the scarcity of jobs. 1 2 3 4 5
26. The best political system for South Africa is one that is based on one person one vote in a unitary state. 1 2 3 4 5
27. The best political system for South Africa is one which is based on a constitution that recognizes minority or group rights in a unitary state. 1 2 3 4 5
28. The best political system for South Africa is one which is based on the partitioning of South Africa into a confederation of states. 1 2 3 4 5
29. After apartheid blacks will seek to avenge themselves for the unfairness they suffered under apartheid laws. 1 2 3 4 5
30. If conditions for blacks do not improve at a satisfactory pace, whites as group may find themselves under attack from frustrated blacks. 1 2 3 4 5
31. If conditions for blacks do not improve, individual whites may find themselves under attack. 1 2 3 4 5
32. Whites may be subject to some form of attack by blacks because of historical differences. 1 2 3 4 5
33. I would support a President of "Colored" descent. 1 2 3 4 5
34. I would support a President of Indian descent. 1 2 3 4 5
35. I would support a President of African descent. 1 2 3 4 5
36. Values held by "Coloreds" and Africans are similar. 1 2 3 4 5
37. Values held by "Coloreds" and Indians are similar. 1 2 3 4 5
38. Values held by Indians and Africans are similar 1 2 3 4 5
39. The various black groups ("Coloreds," Indians, Africans) deserve the right to live in their exclusive areas. 1 2 3 4 5
40. The ideology expressed by the African Nationalist Congress (ANC) is the best for South Africa. 1 2 3 4 5
41. The ideology expressed by the Black Consciousness Movement (BCM) is the best for South Africa. 1 2 3 4 5

42. The ideology expressed by the Conservative Party is the best for South Africa   1 2 3 4 5

43. The ideology expressed by the Democratic Party is the best for South Africa   1 2 3 4 5

44. The ideology expressed by the HNP is the best for South Africa.   1 2 3 4 5

45. The ideology expressed by Inkatha Movement is the best for South Africa.   1 2 3 4 5

46. The ideology expressed by the Labor Party is the best for South Africa.   1 2 3 4 5

47. The ideology expressed by the Natal Indian Congress is the best for South Africa.   1 2 3 4 5

48. The ideology expressed by the Nationalist Party is the best for South Africa.   1 2 3 4 5

49. The ideology expressed by the Pan-Africanist Congress (PAC) is the best for South Africa.   1 2 3 4 5

50. The position adopted by the Tricameral Coalition is the best for South Africa.   1 2 3 4 5

51. The ideology expressed by the United Democratic Front is the best for South Africa.   1 2 3 4 5

52. In a new political dispensation, homeland leaders should give up their leadership to new, and democratically elected leaders.   1 2 3 4 5

53. Homeland leaders will resist giving up their leadership to new and democratically elected leaders.   1 2 3 4 5

54. Within the various black communities ("Colored," Indian, African), educated people see themselves as different from uneducated people.   1 2 3 4 5

55. Within the various black communities ("Colored" Indian, African), the economically well-off people see themselves as different from the less well-off, or poor people.   1 2 3 4 5

56. In the South African situation the struggle for power is mainly between the various race groups.   1 2 3 4 5

57. In the South African situation the struggle for power is mainly between the educated and the uneducated.   1 2 3 4 5

58. In terms of lifestyle, the "Colored" middle-class is quite similar to the Indian middle-class. 1 2 3 4 5

59. In terms of political beliefs, the "Colored" middle-class is quite similar to the Indian middle-class. 1 2 3 4 5

60. In terms of lifestyle, the "Colored" middle-class is quite similar to the African middle-class. 1 2 3 4 5

61. In terms of political beliefs, the "Colored" middle-class is quite similar to the African middle-class. 1 2 3 4 5

62. In terms of lifestyle, the Indian middle-class is quite similar to the African middle-class. 1 2 3 4 5

63. In terms of political beliefs, the Indian middle-class is quite similar to the African middle-class. 1 2 3 4 5

64. Middle-class blacks ("Coloreds," Indians, Africans), fare better than lower-income blacks. 1 2 3 4 5

65. In the event of a conflict, or an uprising middle-class "Coloreds" will align themselves with the ruling government whether black or white. 1 2 3 4 5

66. In the event of a conflict, or an uprising middle-class Indians will align themselves with the ruling government. 1 2 3 4 5

67. In the event of a conflict, or an uprising middle-class Africans will align themselves with the ruling government. 1 2 3 4 5

68. In the event of a conflict, or an uprising middle-class "Coloreds" will align themselves with the disadvantaged people. 1 2 3 4 5

69. In the event of a conflict, or an uprising middle-class Indians will align themselves with the disadvantaged people. 1 2 3 4 5

70. In the event of a conflict, or an uprising middle-class Africans will align themselves with the disadvantaged people. 1 2 3 4 5

71. In terms of the political and economic system, which country serves as the best model for South Africa? Why?

Appendix E
2016–2017 Survey Questionnaire

Demographic Information
In this section a few questions are asked about yourself. Please answer them as precisely as you can.

1. Which province do you live in South Africa?

2. Which city or town? _____

3. Which suburb or township? _____

4. Which languages do you speak? Please rank in order of fluency, from most fluent to least fluent.
    a. _____
    b. _____
    c. _____
    d. _____
    e. _____

5. Age
    a. Less than 21
    b. 21–30
    c. 31–40
    d. 41–50
    e. 51 and above

6. Gender
    a. Female
    b. Male

7. How do you identify yourself?
   a. "Colored"
   b. African
   c. Asian
   d. Nguni
   e. Sotho
   f. Black
   g Other (Specify)_____

ECONOMIC AND POLITICAL IDEOLOGIES

To the following questions please indicate your response in the following manner:

1 = Strongly disagree; 2 = Disagree; 3 = Don't know; 4 = Agree; 5 = Strongly agree.

8. A capitalist/free enterprise economic system will work best for South Africa.   1 2 3 4 5

9. A part-capitalist/part-socialist economic system will work best for South Africa.   1 2 3 4 5

10. A socialist economic system will work best for South Africa.   1 2 3 4 5

11. A communist economic system will work best for South Africa.   1 2 3 4 5

12. Rural people should be discouraged from migrating to urban areas unless jobs can be guaranteed for them.   1 2 3 4 5

13. In urban areas, rural migrants behave better than urban people.   1 2 3 4 5

14. Rural people lower the general standards of living in urban areas.   1 2 3 4 5

15. Urban people view themselves as superior to rural people.   1 2 3 4 5

16. Foreign nationals should be discouraged from migrating to South Africa.   1 2 3 4 5

17. Unless skilled, foreign nationals should be discouraged from migrating to South Africa.   1 2 3 4 5

18. In industrial areas, the most probable cause of conflict is the scarcity of jobs.   1 2 3 4 5

19. In industrial areas, the most probable cause of conflict is strong ethnic affiliations. 1 2 3 4 5

20. For the historically disadvantaged, if conditions do not improve, whites as a group may be targets of hostility. 1 2 3 4 5

21. For the historically disadvantaged, if conditions do not improve, individual whites may be targets of hostility. 1 2 3 4 5

22. Whites may be targets of some form of hostility because of historical political differences. 1 2 3 4 5

23. I would support a President of "Colored" descent. 1 2 3 4 5

24. I would support a President of Indian descent. 1 2 3 4 5

25. I would support a President who is white. 1 2 3 4 5

26. In the event of a conflict, or an uprising middle-class Africans will align themselves with the ruling government. 1 2 3 4 5

27. In the event of a conflict, or an uprising middle-class "Coloreds" will align themselves with the ruling government whether black or white. 1 2 3 4 5

28. In the event of a conflict, or an uprising middle-class Indians will align themselves with the ruling government. 1 2 3 4 5

29. In the event of a conflict, or an uprising middle-class Africans will align themselves with the disadvantaged people. 1 2 3 4 5

30. In terms of the political and economic system, which country serves as the best model for South Africa? Why?

Bibliography

Adam, H., Slabbert, V. & Moodley, K. *Comrades in Business: Post-Liberation Politics in South Africa*. Utrecht, NL: International Books, 2012.
Adam, Heribert and Kogila Moodley. *South Africa without Apartheid*. University Berkeley: University of California Press, 1986.
Adam, Heribert. "Legitimacy and the institutionalization of ethnicity: Comparing South Africa." In *Ethnic Groups and the State*. Edited by Paul Brass.Totowa, New Jersey: Barnes and Noble Books, 1985.
Ajam, T. and Aron, J. Fiscal Renaissance in a Democratic South Africa. *Journal of African Economies*, 16(5): (2007), 745-781.
Alexander, G., Benson, P. and Kampmeyer, J. Investigating the Valuation Effects of Announcements of Voluntary Corporate Selloffs. *Journal of Finance*, 39 (June 1984), 503-517.
Andrews, K. R. *The Concept of Corporate Strategy*. Homewood, IL: Irwin, 1971.
Atkinson, D. "Taking to the Streets: Has Developmental Local Government Failed in South Africa?" In *State of the Nation: South Africa 2007*. Edited by Buhlungu, S., Daniel, J., Southall, R. & Lutchman, J. (Eds.)., pp. 53-77. Cape Town, South Africa: HSRC Press, 2012.
Atrow, Andre. *Zimbabwe: A Revolution That Lost Its Way*? London: Zed Press, 1983.
Avirgan, T. South Africa's economic gap grows wider while Brazil's narrows slightly. EPA Snapshot, www.epi.org/economic snap-shots/entry/ webfeatures_snapshots/entry/websites_20060419, April 9, 2006.
Baker, Pauline. "Facing up to apartheid." *Foreign Policy*. Vol. 64, (Fall 1986), 37–62.
Baran, Paul. *The Political Economy of Growth*. Monthly Review Inc., New York, 1957.
Barnet, Richard J. and Muller, Ronald E. *Global Reach. The Power of the Multinational Corporations*. New York: Simon and Schuster, 1974.
Barth, Fredrik. *Ethnic Groups and Boundaries: The Social Organization of Culture Difference*. Boston: Little, Brown, 1969.

Bendix, Reinhard. *Max Weber. An Intellectual Portrait.* Garden City, New York: Doubleday and Company, Inc., 1960.

Bhana, Surendra, and Bridglal Pachai. Editors. *Cape Town and Johannesburg: A Documentary History Of Indian South Africans.* David Philip Publishers, 1984.

Biko, Steve. *I Write What I Like. A selection of his writings.* Edited by Aelred Stubbs C.R. The Bowerdean Press, 1978.

Bishop, George F, Alfred J. Tuchfarber, Robert W. Oldendick. "Opinions on Fictitious Issues: The Pressure to Answer Survey Questions." *Public Opinion Quarterly,* Vol. 50, 1986, 240–250.

Borger, Julian. "The word "Zapu" vanishes as Zim 's biggest rift heals." *Weekly Mail.* December 15–20, 1989, 18.

Brass, Paul. "Ethnic Groups and the State." In *Ethnic Groups and the State.* Edited by Paul Brass. Totowa, New Jersey:Barnes and Noble Books, 1985, 1–56.

Brown, L.O. and Beik, L.L. *Marketing Research and Analysis.* New York: The Ronald Press Co., 1969.

Butler, Jeffrey, Robert I. Rotberg, and John Adams.*The Black Homelands Of South Africa. The Political And Economic Development Of Bophuthatwana And KwaZulu.* University of California Press, 1977.

Campbell, Horace. "War, Reconstruction and Dependence in Mozambique." *Third World Quarterly.* Vol. 6, Number 4, (October 1984), 839–867.

Carrier, Fred J. *The Third World Revolution.* Amsterdam. B.R. Guner B. V., 1976.

Carroll, A.B. The Pyramid of Corporate Social Responsibility: Toward the Moral Management of Organizational Stakeholders. *Business Horizons.* 34, 4, (1991) 39–48.

Carter, W.B. True Reparations Governing Two Cities: Civil Law and Religious Institutions. *George Washington Law Review.* 68,5/6, (2000), 1021–1034.

Cell, John W. *The Highest Stage Of White Supremacy. The Origins Of Segregation In South Africa And The American South.* Cambridge: University Press, 1982.

Chandler, A.D. *Strategy and Structure: Chapters in the History of the American Industrial Enterprise.* Cambridge, M.I.T. Press, 1982.

Chisholm, L. Apartheid Education Legacies and New Directions in Post-Apartheid South Africa. Storia Delle Donne, 8: 81–103. Retrieved on 3/20/2012 from: http://91.121.146.53/index.php/sdd/article/viewFile/11892/11291, 2012.

Christofides, N., Muirhead, D., Jewkes, R., Penn-Kekana, L. and Conco, N. *Including Post-Exposure Prophylaxis to Prevent HIV/AIDS into Post- Sexual Assault Health Services in South Africa: Costs and Cost Effectiveness of User Preferred Approaches to Provision.* Pretoria: Medical Research Council. Accessed on July 2, 2009 from http://www.uni-cef.org/ southafrica/SAF_resource_violencehivaids pdf, 2006.

Crapanzano, Vincent. *Waiting. The Whites of South Africa.* New York: Vintage Books, 1986.

Crawford, N. and Klotz, A. Editors. *How Sanctions Work: Lessons from South Africa.* London, Macmillan, 1997.

Cronkite, Walter. "Children Of Apartheid." *CBS special,* 1987.

Davidow, Jeffrey. *A peace in Southern Africa: The Lancaster House conference on Rhodesia.* Colorado: Westview Press, 1984.

Davis, Duane and Cosenza, Robert. *Business Research for Decision Making*. Boston: PWS-KENT Publishing Company, 1988.

Deetz, S. *Democracy in an Age of Corporate Colonization: Developments in Communication and the Politics of Everyday Life*. Albany, SUNY Press, 1997.

DOJ&CD (Department of Justice & Constitutional Development): African Charter on Human and Peoples' Rights. Accessed on May 31, 2009. From http://www.doj.gov.za /policy/african%20charter/african charter.htm#pre, c.1997.

Dewey, J. *Experience and education*. New York: Macmillan Publishing, (1938).

Dubow, Saul. Racial Segregation And The Origins Of Apartheid In South Africa, 1919–36. New York: St. Martin's Press, 1989.

Educational Opportunities Council SAEP/SAHEP Participants Report Statistics for 1979–1990.

Fedderke, J.W., De Kadt, R. & Luiz, J.M. Uneducating South Africa: The Failure to Address the 1910–1993 Legacy. *International Review of Education*, 46,3/4 (2000), 257–281.

Ferber, Robert. "Item Non response in a Consumer Survey." *Public Opinion Quarterly*, Vol. 30, (1966), 399–415.

Frank, Andre Gunder. "Political Ironies in the World Economy." *Studies in Political Economy*. Vol. 15, (Fall1984), 119–149.

Freeman, R.E. *Strategic Management: A Stakeholder Approach*. Boston, Pitman, 1984.

Friedman, M. The Social Responsibility of Business Is to Increase Profits. *New York Times Magazine*. (September 13, 1970), 32–33, 122, 126.

Furnivall, J.S. *Netherlands India: A study of a plural economy.* Cambridge, 1944.

Galtung, J.*Theory and Methods of Social Research*. New York: Columbia University Press, 1969.

Geertz, Clifford (editor). "The integrative revolution. Primordial sentiments New York: and civil politics in the new states." *In Old Societies and New States.* New York: Free Press, 1963.

Glazer, Nathan, and Daniel P. Moynihan. *Ethnicity: Theory and Experience*. Cambridge: Harvard University Press, 1975.

Goodpaster, K.E. Business Ethics and Stake Holder Analysis. *Business Ethics Quarterly*, 1,1, (1991), 53–73.

Gurr, Ted. *Why Men Rebel*. Princeton University Press, 1970.

Gutteridge, William. "South Africa: Apartheid 's Endgame." *Conflict Studies*. No. 228, (February 1990), 1–36.

Hani, Chris. A public talk given at UMass/Amherst, May, 1991.

Hart, G. *Disabling Globalization: Places of Power in Post-Apartheid South Africa.* Berkeley, University of California Press, 2002.

Hartshorne, K. *The Making of Education Policy in South Africa*. Cape Town, Oxford University Press Southern Africa, 1999.

Heaven, Patrick C.L. "Ethnic polarization in South Africa: myth or reality?" *Ethnic and Racial Studies*. Vol. 6, Number 3, (July 1983).

Hoagland, Jim. South Africa. *Civilizations In Conflict*. Boston: Houghton Mifflin Company, 1972.

Hoogeveen, J.G. and Ozler, B. "Not Separate, Not Equal: Poverty and Inequality in Post-Apartheid South Africa." *Working Paper #739*. Washington, DC: World Bank, 2005.

Hopkins, J. R. Studying abroad as a form of experiential education. *Liberal Education*, 85(3), 36–41, (1999).

Human Sciences Research Council. Poverty in South Africa. Fact Sheet No. 1. July 26. Accessed on September 4, 2009 from http://www.sarpn. org.za/documents/d0000990/P1096-Fact_Sheet_No_1_Poverty.pdf, 2004.

Jain, P.C. "The Effect of Voluntary Sell-Off Announcements on Shareholder Wealth." *Journal Finance*. 40,1, (1985), 209–224.

Jansen, Jonathan D. "Political Symbolism As Policy Craft: Explaining Non-Reform In South African Education After Apartheid." *Journal of Education Policy*, 17, 2, (2002), 199–215.

Kahn, M.J. "Five Years Gone: A Case Study of Education Policy Implementation in the Transition to Democracy in South Africa." *International Journal of Educational Development*, 16, 3, (1996), 281–289.

Kallaway, P. (editor). The *History of Education under Apartheid 1948–1994*. Cape Town, Maskew Miller Longman, 2002.

Khoza, Reuel J. *Attuned Leadership: Ubuntu Leadership As Compass*. New York: Penguin Books, 2012.

Klein, A. "The Timing and Substance of Divestiture Announcements: Individual, Simultaneous and Cumulative Effects." *Journal of Finance,* 41,3, (1986), 685–696.

Lal, Barbara Ballis. "Perspectives on ethnicity: old wine in new bottles." *Ethnic and Racial Studies*. Vol. 6, Number 2, (April 1983).

Lambert, Bruce. "For Yugoslav-Americans, Partisan Emotions and Worries Over the Bloodshed." *The New York Times International*. Sunday, June 30, 1991, 8.

Leach, Edmund R. "Caste, Class and Slavery: The Taxonomic Problem." *The Logic of Social Hierarchies*. Edited by Edward O. Laumann, Paul M. Siegel, and Robert W. Hodge. Chicago: Markham Publishing Company, 1970.

Lipset, Seymour Martin. *Political Man: The social bases of politics*. London: Heinemann, 1960.

Louw, Leon and Frances Kendall. *South Africa. The solution*. Bisho, Ciskei: Amagi Publication, 1986.

Macionis, John J. *Sociology*. Englewood Cliffs: Prentice-Hall, 1987.

Magdoff, Harry. *Imperialism: From the Colonial Age to the Present*. New York: Monthly Review Press, 1978.

Magubane, Bernard Makhosezwe. *The Political Economy of Race and Class in South Africa*. New York and London: Monthly Review Press, 1979.

Makgoba, Malegapuru, M. (editor). *African Renaissance*. Sandton, Mafube Publishing, Pty. Ltd, 1999.

Malan, Rian. *My Traitor's Heart. A South African Exile Returns To Face His Country, His Tribe, And His Conscience*. New York: The Atlantic Monthly Press, 1990.

Mangaliso, Mzamo P. South Africa: "Corporate Social Responsibility, and the Sullivan Principles." *Journal of Black Studies*, 28, 2, (1997), 219–238.

———. "Building Competitive Advantage from Ubuntu: Management Lessons from South Africa." *Academy of Management Executive*, 15, 3, (2001), 23–35.

———. *The relationship of environmental turbulence, strategy preference and performance. A study of the perceptions of North American and South African corporate executives.* Amherst: Doctoral Dissertation. Amherst. University of Massachusetts, 1988.

———. "The Corporate Social Challenge For The Multinational Corporations." *Journal Of Business Ethics*, Vol. 7, No. 11, (July 1992), 491–500.

Manganyi, Chabani N. "Public Policy and the Transformation of Education in South Africa." In *Implementing Education Policy in South Africa*. Edited by Sayed, Y. & Jansen, J.D., Cape Town, University of Cape Town Press, 2001.

Maodzwa-Taruvinga, M. & Cross, M. "Jonathan Jansen and the Curriculum Debate in South Africa: An Essay Review of Jansen's Writings Between 1999 and 2009," *Curriculum Inquiry,* 42, 1, (2012), 126–152.

Marger, M.N. *Race and Ethnic Relations: American and Global Perspectives*. Belmont, Thomson Wadsworth, 2006.

Marx, Karl. *Capital*. Introduced by Ernest Mandl. Translated by Ben Fowkes. Vol. 1, Vintage Books. New York: Random House, 1972.

Mason, David. "Industrialization, race and class conflict in South Africa: towards a sociological resolution of a reopened debate." *Ethnic and Racial Studies*. Vol. 3 Number 2, (April 1980).

Matossian, M. "Ideologies of Delayed Industrialization." *Economic Development and Cultural Change*. Vol. 6, (April 1958), 217–218.

Mattes, R. "South Africa: Democracy without the People?" *Journal of Democracy*, 13, 1, (2002), 22–36.

Mazrui, Ali A. *The Africans. A Triple Heritage*. Boston: Little, Brown and Company, 1986.

Mbigi, L. & Maree, J. *Ubuntu: The Spirit of African Transformational Management*. Randburg, Knowledge Resources, Inc., 1995.

McClelland, David C. *The Achieving Society*. New Jersey: Van Nostrand, 1961.

McCuen, Gary E. *The Apartheid Reader*. Wisconsin: Gary E. McCuen Publications Inc., 1986.

McFarlin, D.M., Coster, E.A. and Mogale-Pretorius, C. "South African Management Development in the Twenty-First Century: Moving toward an Africanized model." *Journal of Management Development.* 18, 1, (1999), 63–78.

McWilliams, A., Siegel, D. and Teoh, S.H. "Issues in the Use of the Event Study Methodology: A Critical Analysis of Corporate Social Responsibility Studies." *Organizational Research Methods*, 2, 4, (1999), 340–365.

Meznar, M.B., Nigh, D. and Kwok, C.C. "Effect of Announcements of Withdrawal from South Africa on Stockholder Wealth." *Academy of Management Journal*. 37, 6, (1994), 1633–1648.

Milne, R.S. "The Relevence of Ethnicity." *Political Science*. Vol 41, Number 2, (December 1989), 31–50.

Milton, Gordon. *Assimilation in American life. The Role of Race, Religion and National Origins*. New York: Oxford University Press. 1964.

Milward A. S. *The Reconstruction of Western Europe, 1945–51*. London: Methuen, 1984.

Minter, William. "South Africa: Straight Talk on Sanctions." *Foreign Policy*. Vol 65, (Winter 1986–87).

Mnyaka, M. & Motlhabi, M. "The African Concept of *Ubuntu*/Botho and Its Socio-Moral Significance." *Black Theology: An International Journal*, 3, 2, (2005), 215–237.

Mogotlane, Ramaranka, A. "The HIV/AIDS Malady in Southern Africa: Observations from the Epicentre." Keynote Address at the *13th International Conference on Managing in a Global Economy*. Held Rio de Janeiro. June 24, 2009.

Moller, V. South African Quality of Life Trends in the Late 1990s: Major Divides in Perceptions. *Society in Transition*, 30, 2, (1999), 3–105.

Moodie, D.T. *The Rise Of Afrikanerdom Power, Apartheid and the Afrikaner Civil Religion*. Berkerly: University of California Press, 1975.

Moss, Glenn, and Ingrid Obery. (Editors). *South African Review*. Johannesburg: Ravan Press, 1987.

Motlhabi, Mokgethi. *The Theory And Practice Of Black Resistance To Apartheid. A Social-Ethical Analysis*. Johannesburg: Skotaville Publishers, 1987.

Moyo, D. Mediating crisis: Realigning media policy and deployment of propaganda in Zimbabwe, 2000–2008. Edited by S. Chiumbu & M. Musemwa. In *Crisis! What Crisis? The Multiple Dimensions of the Zimbabwean Crisis*, pp. 176–198. Pretoria, HSRC Press, (2012).

Mutwa, Credo, Vusa 'mazulu. *My People, My Africa*. New York: The John Day Company, 1969.

Nelson, Harold D. (Editor). *South Africa. A Country Study*. Library of Congress Cataloging in Publication Data, 1981.

Ngassam, C. An Examination of Stock Market Reactions to U.S. Corporate Divestitures in South Africa. Montclair State University, NJ: Center for Economic Research on Africa, Accessed on July 9, 2009 from: ftp://ftp.cba.uri.edu/classes/dash/fin625/StkRet-DivestSA.pdf, 1992.

Nyquist, Thomas E. *African Middle-Class Elite*. Institute of Social and Economic Research. Grahamstown: Rhodes University, 1983.

Oler, D.K., Harrison, J. S. and Allen, M. R. "The Danger of Misinterpreting Short-Window Event Study Findings in Strategic Management Research: An Empirical Illustration Using Horizontal Acquisitions." *Strategic Organization*, 6, 2, (2008), 151–184.

Olzak, Susan. "Contemporary Ethnic Mobilization." *Annual Review of Sociology*. Vol 9. (1983), 355–374.

Orkin, Mark. *Disinvestment, The Struggle, and the Future. What Black South Africans Really Think*. Johannesburg: Raven Press, 1986.

Osagae, Eghosa E. "Redeeming The Utility Of The Ethnic Perspective In African Studies: Towards A New Agenda." *The Journal of Ethnic Studies*, Vol 18, No. 2, (Summer 1990), 37–58.

Özler, B. "Not Separate, Not Equal: Poverty and Inequality in Post-apartheid South Africa." *Economic Development and Cultural Change*, 55, 3, (2007), 487–529.

Pachai, B. *The International Aspects Of The South African Indian Question 1860–1971.* Cape Town: C. Struik Pty Ltd., 1971.
Patel, F. "SA Education System Ranked One of the Worst in World." Cii News & Agencies, 13 September. Retrieved on 3/20/2013 from: www.ciibroadcasting.com/2012/09/13, 2012.
Payer, Cherly. *The Debt Trap: The International Monetary Fund and the Third World.* Monthly Review Press, 1974.
Peires, J.B. *The House Of Phalo. A History Of The Xhosa People In The Days Of Their Independence.* Berkerley: University of California Press, 1981.
Pinkney, Alphonso. *The Myth of Black Progress.* Cambridge: Cambridge University Press, 1987.
Poe, Gail, Isadore Seeman, Joseph McLaughlin, Eric Mehl, Michael Dietz. "Don't Know Boxes in Factual Questions in a Mail Questionnaire. Effects on Level and Quality of Response." *Public Opinion Quarterly*, Vol. 52 (1988) 212–222.
Pomeroy, William J. *Apartheid, Imperialism and African Freedom.* New York: International Publishers, 1986.
Posnikoff, J.F. "Disinvestment from South Africa: They Did Well by Doing Good." *Contemporary Economic Policy.* 15, 1, (1997), 76–86.
Prinsloo, E.D. "The African View of Participatory Business Management." *Journal of Business Ethics*, 25, 4, (2000), 275–286.
Rabushka, Alvin and Kenneth A Shepsle. *Politics in Plural societies. A Theory of Democratic Instability.* Columbus: A Bell & Howell Company, 1972.
Ramose, M.B. *African Philosophy through Ubuntu.* Harare, Mond Books, 1999.
Randall, D.J. Prospects for the Development of a Black Business Class in South Africa. *Journal of Modern African Studies*, 34, 4, (1996), 661–686.
Robertson, Ian. *Sociology.* New York: Worth Publishers, 1987.
Rotberg, Robert I. "Seven Scenarios for South Africa," in *South Africa: In Transition to What?* Edited by Helen Kitchen.Washington, D.C.: Center for Strategic and International Studies, 1988.
Rothchild, Donald. "Interethnic conflict and policy analysis in Africa." *Ethnic and Racial Studies.* Vol. 9, No. 1, (January 1986), 67–86.
SAIRR. *South African Survey: 2002–2003.* Johannesburg, South African Institute of Race Relations, 2003.
Schlemmer, Lawrence. "Privilege, prejudice and parties: A study of patterns of political motivation among white voters in Durban." *Institute of Race Relations*, Johannesburg, 1973.
Sechaba. An African National Congress Monthly Publication. May 1989.
Setiloane, G.M. *African Theology: An Introduction.* Johannesburg, Skotaville Publishers, 1986.
Sheatsley, "Questionnaire Construction and Item Writing," in *Handbook of Survey Research.* Edited by Peter H. Rossi, James D. Wright, Andy B. Anderson. Academic Press, Inc., 1983.
Shils, Edward. "Primodial, Personal, Sacred and Civil Ties: Some Particular Observations on the Relationships of Sociological Research and Theory," *British Journal of Sociology*, Vol. 8, No.2, (June 1957).

Shutte, A. *Ubuntu: An Ethic for a New South Africa*. Pietermaritzburg, Cluster Publications, 2001.
Sithole, Masipula. "Ethnicity and factionalism in Zimbabwe National politics 1957–79." *Ethnic and Racial Studies*. Vol. 3, Number 1, (January 1980).
Skinner, Elliot P. "Competition Within Ethnic Systems in Africa," in *Ethnicity and Resource Competition in Plural Societies*. Edited by Leo Despres. The Hague: Moutoun Publishers, 1975.
Slovo J. "No Middle Road," in *Southern Africa: The New Politics of Revolution*. Edited by B. Davidson, J. Slovo and A.R. Wilkinson. Penguin Books, 1976.
Small, Stephen, A. *Racial Differentiation in the Slave Era: A Comparative Study of People of "Mixed-Race" in Jamaica and Georgia*. Doctoral Dissertation. University of California at Berkely, 1989.
Smolicz, J. J. "Tradition, core values and intercultural development in plural societies." *Ethnic and Racial Studies*. Vol. 11, No. 4, (November 1988), 389–409.
Söderblom, J.D. "Gini Coefficients: Their Role and Operation." World International Community Experts. Accessed on September 15, 2009 from http://world-ice.com/Articles/Gini Coefficients.pdf, 2005.
"South Africa Now." New York: A Public Television News Documentary run by the African National Congress, 1989.
Southall, R. "The ANC & Black Capitalism in South Africa." *Review of African Political Economy*, 3, 100, (2004), 313–328.
Stadler, Alf. *The Political Economy Of Modern South Africa*. London and Sydney: Croom Helm, 1987.
Stokes, R. G. "Afrikaner Colonialism and Economic Action: The Weberian Thesis in South Africa." *American Journal of Sociology*, Vol., 81, (July 1975), 62–81.
Stokes, R.G. and Harris A. "South African Development and the Paradox of Racial Particularism: Towards a Theory of Modernization from the Center." *Economic Development and Cultural Change*, Vol., 26, No. 2, (January 1978), 245–269.
Suckling, John and Landeg White (Editors). *After Apartheid. Renewal of the South African Economy*. New Jersey: Africa World Press, 1988.
Sudman, Seymour. "Applied Sampling," *in Handbook of Survey Research*. Edited by Peter H. Rossi, James D. Wright, Andy B. Anderson. New York: Academic Press, Inc., 1983.
SWAPO. *To Be Born A Nation. The Liberation Struggle for Namibia*. London: Zed Press, 1981.
The Economist. A Survey Of South Africa. November 3, 1990.
The PAC Manifesto Abrigded, 1962.
The Report of the Study Commission on U.S. Policy Toward Southern Africa. *South Africa: Time Running Out*. University of California Press, 1981.
The Wall Street Journal, International. "South Africa's Emigration Trend." Wednesday, July 24, 1991, p. A6.
Thompson, Leonard. *A History Of South Africa*. New Haven: Yale University Press, 1990.
Transparency International. "The Global Coalition against Corruption." Retrieved on 3/22/2012 from http://www.transparency.org/research/cpi/cpi_2012.

Tull, D.S. and Hawkins, D.L. *Marketing Research Meaning, Measurement and Method*. New York: MacMillan, 1976.

UNAIDS. "Overview of the Global Aids Epidemic." *2006 Report on the Global AIDS Epidemic*. Accessed on September 1, 2009 from http://data.unaids.org/pub/Global-Report/2006/2006_GR_CH02_en.pdf, 2006.

Ungar, New York: Sanford J. *Africa. The people and politics of an emerging continent*. New York: Simon and Schuster, 1985.

Valera-Guinot, Helena. "The legalization of the Spanish Communist Party. Elites, Public Opinion, and Symbols in the Spanish Transition."*International Journal of Political Economy. A Journal of Translations*. Vol., 2, (Summer 1990) 28–46.

van den Berghe, Pierre. "Class, race and ethnicity in Africa." *Ethnic and Racial Studies*. 1983.

vander Zanden. *Social Psychology*. New York: Random House, New York.

Waddock, S.A. and Graves, S.B. The Corporate Social Performance-Financial Performance Link. *Strategic Management Journal*, 18, 3, (1997), 303–319.

Washington, Joseph, R. (editor). *Dilemmas Of The New Black Middle Class*. 1980.

Weber, Max. *The Protestant ethic and the spirit of capitalism*. Translated by Talcott Parsons. New York: Scribners, 1930.

Weeks, Joh R. *Population: An Introduction to Concepts and Issues*. 12th edition. Boston. Cangage Learning, 2016.

Whiteside, A. and Sunter, C. *AIDS: The Challenge for South Africa*. Tafelberg: Human and Rousseau, 2000.

Wilson, Francis, and Mamphela Ramphele. *Uprooting Poverty. The South African Challenge*. New York: W.W. Norton and Company, 1989.

Wolpe, Harold. *Race, Class and The Apartheid State*. Paris: Unesco Press, 1988.

Wood, D.J. "Social Performance Revisited." *Academy of Management Review*, 16, 4, (1991), 691–718.

Woods, Donald, and Mike Bostock. *Apartheid. A Graphic Guide*. New York: Henry Holt and Company, 1986.

Woolard, I. "An Overview of Poverty and Inequality in South Africa." *Working Paper Prepared for DFID (SA)*. Accessed on September 2009 from: www.sarpn.org.za/CountryPovertyPapers/SouthAfrica/july2002/woolard/Poverty_Inequality_SA.pdf, 2002. World Bank 2002. Accessed on August 31 2009 from: www.worldbank.org/

Wren, Christopher. "Mandela Release Does Not Halt Fracticide In Natal." *The New York* Times International. Sunday, Feb 25, 1990, 16.

———. "South Africans Divided Over Scandal's Damage To Inkatha." *The New York Times International*. Saturday, August 3, 1991, 21.

———. "Even in New South Africa" Apartheid's Legacy Lives On." *The New York Times*, Sunday, June 23, 1991, 1.

———. "Scandal Threatens de Klerk and Talks." *The New York Times International*. Sunday, July 21, 1991, 3.

———. "Most Powerful Zulu: Charismatic Chief South Africans Either Love or Hate." *The New York Times International*. Wednesday, April 18, 1990, A6.

Wright, P. and Ferris, S.P. "Agency Conflict and Corporate Strategy: The Effect of Divestment on Corporate Value." *Strategic Management Journal.* 18, (1997), 77–83.

Yaukey, David. *Demography: The Study of Human Populations.* Ilinois. Waveland Press Inc., 1990.

Zaltman, G., and Burger, P.C. *Marketing Research: Fundamentals and Dynamics.* Illinois: The Dryden Press, 1975.

Zenner, Walter P. "Arabic-Speaking Immigrants in North America as Middleman Minorities." *Ethnic and Racial Studies.* Vol.5, No. 4, 457–477.

Index

Africans, 2, 72, 123
Afrikaners, 2, 10–15, 31–33
alignments, 81–83
African Nationalist Congress, 55, 80, 88, 101, 119, 121, 128
apartheid government, 16, 24, 37, 39, 72, 92, 112

Bantustan, 3
Black Consciousness Movement, 17, 34, 55, 119, 121, 128
Biko, 37, 55
Boer, 2, 11–13, 15
Boshoff, 32
Britain, 14, 33, 35, 87, 91, 98, 126
British Isles, 87
Broederbond, 14
Buthelezi, 36–38, 43

Calvinism, 13–14
Canada, 87, 91, 105–106, 126
capitalism, 28, 60–61, 86, 88, 97, 105
communism, 60–61
compartmentalization, 29
Cuba, 80, 86, 91
culture, 7, 10, 16, 19, 29, 38, 58

De Klerk, 24, 39, 79
deference, 8, 61

democracy, 1, 5, 23, 29, 34, 60, 90, 92
descent, 7, 10, 16, 33, 61, 66–69, 75, 88, 91

emigration, 33
endogamous marriages, 17
English, 10–11, 13–16, 20, 31–32

homelands, 3, 20, 29, 52, 77–79, 87, 91
hostility, 26, 42, 61–63, 75, 88, 90–91, 102–103, 119, 133

ideology, 2, 31, 33, 36, 41, 43, 54–58, 73–74, 86, 101, 118, 128–129
independence, 4, 6, 13, 15–16, 20, 23, 25, 27–29, 37, 42, 87, 89, 98, 105, 109
Indians, 2, 7, 9, 11, 17–19, 20–21, 36, 39, 47, 55, 58, 64, 67
Inkatha ka Zulu, 37

Mandela, 38, 40, 43, 101, 118
Mass Democratic Movement, 34
Max Weber, 7
minority, 10, 16–17, 32, 35, 39, 43, 58, 82, 86, 92, 104, 118, 128
mixed economy, 28, 34, 58, 60, 74–75, 90, 97, 105

Mixed-Race, 11, 16, 21, 53, 54–55, 57–59, 62, 64–65, 67–68, 72, 74, 78, 81–84, 87
model, 8, 77, 84–87, 91, 93, 95–96, 103–106, 115, 130, 133
Muslims, 64

Ncome River, 12

Pan Africanist Congress, 24, 34, 55

socialism, 28, 60–61, 86–88, 105

United Democratic Front, 34, 39, 43, 55, 57, 121, 129

About the Author

Nomazengele A. Mangaliso is professor of Sociology at Westfield State University. In past years she has served as Chair of the Department of Sociology. She has a Bachelor's degree from the University of Fort Hare, South Africa, a Master's degree from Cornell University, Ithaca New York, and a Ph.D. from the University of Massachusetts at Amherst.

Dr. Mangaliso has taught several courses including Principles of Sociology, Classical Sociological Theory, Race and Ethnic Relations, Collective Behavior and Social Movements, Population Studies in Society, Complex Organizations, and Sociology of Gender. She has presented at several professional meetings including the American Sociological Association, American Political Science Association, and the American Studies Association. She has several chapter publications including "Cultural Boycotts against South Africa," "Gender and Nation Building," "South African and African American Women Journey to Freedom," "Spaces in the Social Order: South African and African American Women's Resistance Movements."

Dr. Mangaliso currently resides in Amherst Massachusetts with her husband the writer of the preface of this book, and faculty member at the Isenberg School of Management at the University of Massachusetts/Amherst. She and her husband have two adult daughters, Bande who resides in Georgia with her family, and Unati who resides in California.

www.ingramcontent.com/pod-product-compliance
Ingram Content Group UK Ltd.
Pitfield, Milton Keynes, MK11 3LW, UK
UKHW020033040426
469671UK00005B/33